STUCK
WHERE
YOU
ARE

(and more fortunate than you know)

Alan Robert Neal

For information about this title or to order additional books and/or electronic media, please visit StuckWhereYouAre.com.

ISBN Print: 978-0615815541

First edition
MFFR-2013-05-12

Structure and editing guidance provided by Scott Barry.

Contents

Preface

The villains of our nightmares
       exist outside our dreams.

They taunt us from within
       even while we are awake.

They must be villains
       else why would they shout?

Perhaps it's because we won't listen.

Acknowledgments

Thank you to my family
who are my close friends.

(The ones still here and those I dearly miss.)

And thank you to my close friends
who are my family.

A special thank-you to Breck Costin.

Introduction

Simon was an engineer for a Silicon Valley think tank. He loved his job. Every day was filled with something new. He would go into a lab, experiment with the latest technologies, and operate ever-changing prototypes.

There was just one problem. Every time Simon sat down in front of a new piece of equipment or experimented with brand-new software, he would start perspiring, and a thought would pop into his head...

> "What if this is the one? What if this is the one that I won't be able to figure out, and everyone will know how stupid I am?"

It didn't matter that Simon's fear was completely unwarranted. It didn't matter that he always learned new devices quickly. And it didn't matter that he never forgot what he learned. For some reason, his unreasonable concern persisted.

Eventually, Simon stopped trying to fight it. He accepted the prerecorded message as part of his morning ritual. There was no surprise. He knew when the recording would start. He knew when it would end. Simon even knew he would learn whatever he needed to learn despite what the recording feared.

Every time Simon heard the recording, he slightly bobbed his head and moved his lips as if he were singing along with a song.

The technique worked perfectly. Simon was able to hear the concern without alarm. He stopped perspiring. And he was able to get on with his day. Eventually, the ritual became so internalized that Simon barely noticed it.

Several years later, Simon left his employer and became an independent consultant. His impressive background was attractive to an incalculable number of technology companies.

Simon loved consulting. It was even more exciting than his previous job. Instead of experiencing the innovations of a single company, he was flying around the world and encountering the innovations of hundreds of brilliant inventors.

There was just one problem. Every time Simon would interview with a new client and see what they were working on, he would think...

> "Wow, look at what they have accomplished. I wonder if I will be able to make a contribution.
>
> "Maybe not. In fact, given the direction of this technology, I wonder how long I'll be needed as a consultant."

In short order, Simon recognized what was happening.

> "This is amazing," he said to himself one day. "Not only have I talked myself out of being able to take on this particular client. In fifteen seconds, I've talked myself out of my entire career."

That's when Simon matched his present-day behavior to his previous ritual.

> "It's the same thing!" he shouted internally to himself. "It's the same music with different lyrics."

Simon was right. Our patterns persist. Our manifestations can change. The words we say might be different. But the music is the same.

That's an interesting thing to know, right? But that's not why I am telling you this story.

Simon eventually recognized that despite the different lyrics, the music was the same. That single melody was playing inside of him. But just like they teach in AA, *everyone* in the meeting is an alcoholic. At the beginning, new people want to think they're different.

> "That guy drinks an entire bottle of vodka every day? That's crazy. I just drink a couple of six-packs."

Right. That's different. Really?

We all need to recognize that our music isn't much different from everyone else's, even when our lyrics are different.

This book is filled with stories of people, their behaviors, and their struggles. You might not think they apply to you. But they do. In every case cited, you have done your own version of the same thing. You just might have chosen a different manifestation. Or maybe you just didn't notice.

If you want to get some value from this book, make it your job to see how you are similar to every single person. How you can feel what they must be feeling. How you can understand why they have done what they have done. See what you do that's similar, even if it's not identical.

If you can manage to get through this book and not make those associations, then you will have succeeded in discovering your problem.

I'm going to cheat and steal a summary from an upcoming chapter. It's worth noting and repeating.

You might be great, but you're not so special.

You might be wounded, but you're not unique.

Be thankful for that.

We are all the same. Some are luckier. Some are not. Some are blessed with more abundant gifts. Some are not.

As it is in a game of cards, our job is to do the best with what we have been dealt. Wishing for new cards or pretending we don't have the ones we have won't help. You can try. You can cheat. You can attempt to leave the game. But as you should know by now, those solutions never last very long.

At a minimum, you were able to afford this book. How great is that? You've got some money.

Or a friend gave it to you. That's wonderful. You have someone who cares.

I suppose you could have stolen the book. Well, if that's the case, maybe you can learn something. Then you could clean up your act and make amends.

If you do nothing other than discovering some of your blessings and putting them to good use, then it's a good day.

You cannot take credit for your blessings. But you can certainly commit to not f——ing them up.

Amputating?

"How do I change it?" Monica begged.

"Change what?"

"That thing... that thing you said I am," Monica emphatically replied.

"Well, that 'thing' you're talking about is part of who you are."

"I don't like that part of myself," Monica declared. "I want it gone!"

What chance do you have of feeling good about yourself when you keep wanting to amputate parts of who you are?

Not all of our behaviors are healthy or even convenient. But that doesn't mean they should be jettisoned without exploration.

We say we want to be loved for who we are. But in most cases, by "who we are", we mean "who we wish we were".

On the following pages, you will be introduced to many people. They all have struggles. Those struggles are rooted in their desperate attempts to not be themselves, although many of them would tell you otherwise.

Ironically, what we see as our detriments are usually our greatest assets.

If you could back off the judgment for just a bit, you would have a chance to notice that.

What parts of yourself are you attempting to amputate?

_____

Are you sure they don't have any value?

_____

Embrace all of your selves.

Uncommitted?

Jean began smoking in her late teens. She had always enjoyed the ritual of methodically pulling the cellophane tab around a newly purchased pack of cigarettes. She liked the feel of the cigarette in her hand, gently tapping it on a table and elegantly lighting it as if she were in a fifties movie. She especially enjoyed the sensation of moving in slow motion, as slowly as the magically floating smoke rings she gently blew between puffs.

One day, while in her mid-thirties, after eighteen years of smoking, Jean decided to stop. And so she did. She simply put down her cigarettes for good. No books. No programs. She just stopped smoking.

When asked how she accomplished her feat, Jean nonchalantly replied...

> "I was done. I didn't like how I smelled. I didn't like being run by my compulsion. I didn't like that I was addicted. I had no choice but to stop if I wanted to start respecting myself.
>
> "But I'll tell you this... I never realized that *not* doing something was so much harder than doing something."

Of course, not everyone can just stop smoking like Jean did. But her point is still valid.

Our salvation is not so much in what we need to do as much as it is in what we need to stop doing. Stop smoking. Stop overeating. Stop drinking. Stop resisting. Stop pretending. Stop fantasizing. Stop numbing yourself. And so on. It's all in what we stop.

Jean demonstrated discipline well beyond what many might be able to muster. And her approach was simple and without unnecessary complication. Could she have explored a variety of theories and bought a bunch of books? Yep. Could she have found more steps to take? Definitely. Was it necessary? Nope.

That's not to say more information isn't valuable to some. I'm only saying that too much information isn't necessarily a good thing or a guarantee for success.

I could not begin to tally the number of people I have met who have spent countless years and dollars jumping at every theory, technique, and fad under the sun. They're no different from those who are slaves to exercise and diet fads. The ones with gym memberships they never use, treadmills they end up selling on Craigslist, and food supplements from every infomercial they see. And yet they have no long-lasting success.

In reality, those who have pursued the widest variety of approaches in trying to rid themselves of undesired behaviors are no more successful — in fact, they are usually less successful — than those who just stopped what they needed to stop.

You might wonder...

"Doesn't it need to be more complex?"

Well, it could be more complex. You can make life as complex as you want. But here's something you could ask yourself: "Has complexity ever helped me in the past?"

And besides, when we are stuck in a cycle of bad behavior or lack of success, it's not because of what we don't know. It's because of what we don't *want* to know.

We keep looking for more palatable solutions. Something not so inconvenient. Something that doesn't require so much work. Something that doesn't force us to drop beliefs we don't want to forsake. And in our quest, we conveniently get to avoid what we already know we should be doing.

For those who think that variety, complexity, and difficulty offer assurances of success, you should know they don't. The only thing that guarantees success is commitment.

Not just any commitment. Commitment to the right thing.

Jean was able to muster discipline on her own. That's fantastic. But that's not a slight toward people who need additional assistance. It's a comment on Jean's commitment.

If Jean had sought additional assistance and made that work, she would have been displaying exactly the same commitment. She was going to do whatever it took to stop smoking. That's what counts.

If Jean tried one technique and it didn't work, she could try another. That's still commitment. But if Jean was trying technique after technique and none of them were working, it wouldn't be a comment on the techniques. It would be a sign of Jean's lack of commitment.

Commitment to the right thing. If a pursuit is working for you *overall*, then it's the right thing.

When I say "overall", I am referring to your health in general. The big picture. For instance, drinking alcohol might help you forget your problems, but overall, it's unhealthy.

If you can get some assistance from this book, that would be wonderful.

Perhaps reading about others will help you realize that you are not alone. Perhaps you will gain more acceptance for yourself. Perhaps the questions at the end of every chapter will help you move forward.

Or perhaps you will simply discover and accept that you need assistance outside yourself. That realization would be equally wonderful.

We all need partners. We should never listen to just ourselves nor limit our input to people who are just like us.

I can never be on the receiving end of my own handshake. I don't know the experience others have of me. I need others to tell me. And if I trust them, I need to listen to what they say.

For instance...

I remember my phone ringing as I walked into my house. A buddy was calling from the street where we had just parted ways.

> "I was watching you walk up the stairs," he began. "And I was thinking about what a sweet and gentle man you are."

I started crying. I had always thought of myself as oversensitive. And I had never considered that I was wrong.

It never occurred to me that my emotional sensitivity would be respected by other men. Especially someone whom most would readily recognize as an alpha male.

I had always been embarrassed by my sensitivity. I thought it was a weakness. I would have never guessed it was one of my greatest virtues.

I had a choice at that moment. Would I keep listening to myself or accept someone else's view instead?

Would I stay committed to what I had always believed or be open to what the world was telling me?

It's very easy to commit to the wrong perspective. In fact, that's what most stuck people do. They come up with conclusions, and they stick to them.

Remember the tombstone of the hypochondriac:

"I told you I was sick."

Perhaps that person really was sick. On the other hand, maybe they were willing to sacrifice whatever it took because they were more committed to being right than they were to their own well-being.

How about you?

Which one are you committed to?

On a scale of 1 to 10, what's your commitment to discovering who you really are as opposed to fighting for who you wish you were?

_____

What unhealthy behaviors are keeping you stuck?

_____

Commit to your health.

Prejudiced?

When Chuck was a kid, his adenoids were infected. So the doctors took them out. They also grabbed Chuck's tonsils. Two for the price of one. Back then, doctors thought tonsils were unnecessary, so what the heck.

Turned out that conventional wisdom was wrong. Tonsils do have a benefit. But because the benefit had not been observed, it was assumed that it did not exist.

What if the same is true for all of those seemingly negative thoughts in your head? The ones you hate. What if they have unseen benefits? What if those negative thoughts, just like tonsils, are actually essential? Would you still want to get rid of them?

"Not so fast," you protest.

I couldn't be talking about *your* thoughts. Yours are really bad. Not like everyone else's.

Well, maybe that's true. There certainly are some people who need assistance beyond what any book can provide. This book isn't for people who need professional care. If you do need it, then please take care of yourself and seek it.

This book is for the people who truly are fine as they are, but don't like their circumstances. Those who are trying to rid themselves of pesky thoughts of self-doubt. Those whose day-to-day lives are constantly interrupted by those thoughts. Those who buy self-help books and attend seminars in search of the perfect mantra.

Perhaps you are worried that nothing you have tried has worked. Those dark thoughts are still with you. Making you feel insecure and depressed.

Sometimes they go away, but then they come back with a vengeance. Strong as ever. Defiant. Even brazen. And you're hoping that maybe this is the book. Maybe, once and for all, you will be able to purge those thoughts from your head.

If only there was a way to cleanse those thoughts. Who wouldn't jump at the opportunity? Who would blame you?

You have been searching your entire adult life. Maybe even longer. You have read articles. You've talked to people. You picked up this book, hoping it would help. And you're not alone. For years, psychologists, psychiatrists, self-help gurus, magazines, and newspapers have told you that you should purge yourself of negative thoughts. They advocate...

"Think positive."

But what if they're wrong?

In any interaction, whether it's in school, in an office, in a neighborhood, on a sports team, etc., there are always inconvenient personalities, perspectives, and thoughts. It's tempting to dump them. But also...

There's a good chance that many of your thoughts, no matter the difficulties they often present, also have some worthwhile perspectives to offer. They have contributions to make.

Think of the neighborhood gossip. Maybe she's annoying as hell, but at least she makes an awesome chocolate-chip cookie.

In the end, a team is stronger for involving all of its players, especially when each member is playing in the correct position.

What if your prejudice is unfounded?

What if your internal team members — those thoughts — have more value than you could have ever imagined?

What if, for all of these years, you had simply been playing them in the wrong position?

Still wanna kill 'em off?

What prejudice do you have against certain parts of yourself?

_____

Are you open to the possibility that every single part of you might have value?

_____

If not, is there any reason to continue reading?

_____

**Find value in the parts of yourself
you currently hate.**

Fatalistic?

"WAAAAAIT!" she screamed at the top of her lungs. "Don't cross the streeeeeeeet! You're going to get HIT. You're going to DIE!"

Suzie stopped dead in her tracks. She looked around. No one was there.

"Damn it," she muttered in frustration. "I fell for it again."

Whenever you cross a street, whether physical or emotional, there is a possibility that you might get hit by a car. Whenever you try something, there is always a possibility that you will fail.

To some degree, your awareness of bad possibilities can keep you safe. It can keep you from getting hit by a car and from failing.

But taken too far, the awareness can paralyze you. So much so that you might not ever cross a street or try anything outside your comfort zone.

Suzie grew up with her parents foretelling awful events. They made their case by alleging Suzie's deficiencies.

"You're so naïve," they would tell her.

If Suzie doubted herself, then she would believe whatever her parents said. The strategy worked. Suzie was racked with doubt.

Maybe Suzie's parents were motivated by their own fear. Maybe they were jealous of her potential. Maybe they were just nasty. Or maybe they were shortsighted. It doesn't matter because their negativism had done the damage.

There is a chance that most everything you have ever been told is true or will be true. Of course, there is also a possibility that it is not true and will not be true. So what should you do?

Should you avoid crossing emotional intersections because you fear the risk of getting hit or failing? You'll never get anywhere.

Should you take another route? It might not lead to where you want.

Should you ignore the possibility of getting hit and cross as if nothing was there? That could be lethal.

For every statement that Suzie heard while growing up, a permanent thought... a perspective... an internal voice was assigned inside her head.

> "You're naïve."

Suzie was a kid. She couldn't know who and what was credible, and who and what wasn't. So every thought, every perspective, had the same rank.

Every time Suzie heard a particular statement or anything similar, the corresponding internal voice grew louder.

> **"YOU'RE FOOLISH!"**
>
> **"YOU'RE STUPID!"**
>
> **"YOU'LL NEVER AMOUNT TO ANYTHING!"**

In short order, the thoughts that Suzie heard internally were identical to those she had heard externally. The voices now lived inside her head.

Suzie couldn't wait to leave home. But where could she go?

After all, she was so naïve, so foolish, and so stupid. Everyone said that about her.

By the time she was five, Suzie was saying that about herself.

And so Suzie's perspective — the perspective of a five-year-old — distorts her view, her actions, and her future.

What fatalistic thoughts did you absorb growing up?

_____

Whom did these thoughts come from?

_____

How many negative predictions came to pass?

_____

Which thoughts do you still believe?

_____

Note the predictions that have never come true.

Misled?

When Buzz was a kid, there was nothing he could do to please his parents. If he won a competition, his parents would say, "It must have been easy." If he came in second place, they told him he must not have tried hard enough.

Whatever Buzz did wasn't adequate. Or so he was told. Buzz believed the message and thought that he wasn't enough.

Throughout childhood, adolescence, and adulthood, Buzz became ultra-responsible and taught himself an insanely diverse number of expert skills. That's a good way to be, right?

Well, yes and no. It's great to be a responsible person; people love that. It's wonderful to have a wide variety of expert skills; they come in handy.

But it's not so good if you are burdened by feeling responsible for things that are outside of your control. It's not a good thing if you interpret every problem around you as your own personal failure.

And it's also not a good thing to seek approval from people who are so disappointed in their own lives that they are unable to treat you kindly.

Buzz's first conclusion was that he wasn't enough. That was a problem. A problem he intended to fix.

But Buzz was wrong. He was enough.

Our oldest observations are the ones we had when we were children. And our strongest, even sacred, conclusions are the ones that were borne out of the pain.

We usually decide two things: What we will do to fix ourselves. And what we will never or always do to other people.

For example...

> "I'm going to make lots of money."

> "I'm going to leave this place."

> "I'm going to be rich and famous."

> "I'll show them."

> "I'll never treat the people I love this way."

> "I'll never yell at my kids."

Our motivations are legitimate. Wanting to be safe, loved, and treated kindly is reasonable and healthy. But our observations, conclusions, and strategies are not well formed at those early ages. How could they be?

What was the problem with Buzz's original observations? He had no experience outside of his family. At a young age, they were the only people he lived with. And so his observations lacked context.

What was the other problem with Buzz's original observation? He thought his parents were disappointed in him for not being enough. In reality, his parents were disappointed with everything.

What was the problem with Buzz's conclusion? He went for the insurmountable. He thought there was something he could do to garner his parents' approval. There wasn't. It was never his problem in the first place.

If Buzz had more insight, he might have noticed that nothing was ever enough for his parents. It had nothing to do with him.

With more perspective, Buzz might have concluded that he was always enough. Instead of obsessively driving himself to an unattainable perfection, he could have realized that he just needed to find people who would appreciate what he could offer and not criticize him for what he could not.

But we gather other perspectives as we grow up, right? Well, yes and no.

Buzz was surely the recipient of appreciation as he grew older. If not in his early childhood, then later in life. He did receive kindness, and he collected other perspectives.

But the positive things Buzz heard were not enough to alter his original observations or conclusions. Why is that?

Imagine you were told something when you were five. Every day of your life, you were repeatedly told the same thing. You believe it.

At age fifteen, someone tells you something different. It's a fluke —right?— because it's inconsistent with everything else you have been told about yourself. So you don't believe it.

You want to believe the positive things you're hearing. But every time you try, you're reminded of what you were told in the past.

Besides that, it's not all in the past. You're still hearing the negatives from the original perpetrators.

You continue on. Maybe you move out of the house. Luckily, you continue hearing that other point of view. Finally, you believe it or at least believe that it could be true. Problem solved, right?

Nope, the problem is not solved. That's because your other perspectives — the observations you had at age five — still exist. In fact, the originals have at least a decade's worth of seniority over the newer information.

In other words, the new perspectives are always junior to the original ones, which are etched deeper into your being.

The longer the time between your first childhood observations and whatever else you hear, the greater the seniority of your original observations.

It doesn't matter that your original observations were never right. They're still there.

If your observations weren't right, then what are the chances that your conclusions were?

Without discernment, your life is being run by the observations and conclusions of a five-year-old.

And if that is the case, you are being misled.

How are your childhood observations misleading you today?

_____

What conclusions did you reach?

_____

Which of those conclusions, if any, have you properly questioned?

_____

Distinguish between the solvable and unsolvable.

Misdiagnosed?

As a skinny kid with an ever-growing lack of confidence, Rudy always felt unsafe and unsure of himself. He felt taunted, in danger, and stupid.

To Rudy, everything was an assault. And it was always personal. If a kid shoved him in the lunch line, they were calling him weak. If someone pushed him on the bus, they were calling him lame. If a jock ignored him, they were calling him a punk.

Most of the time, the other kids were just being kids, doing what kids do. But to Rudy, every playful and thoughtless interaction was an act of aggression. Kids do of course say nasty things to one another, but Rudy didn't notice that. He only noticed when he was the recipient.

Rudy's feelings grew worse during his teens. As a young adult, he turned to drugs.

The drugs didn't help, so Rudy decided to become a bodybuilder. Surely, bigger muscles would solve the problem and make him feel safe.

Within a short time, Rudy nearly doubled his size, but it wasn't enough. He still felt unsafe.

So he learned to fight. But he thought it wasn't enough. "What if multiple bullies attack me?"

So he learned how to use weapons. They weren't enough. "What if I'm mugged?"

So he started carrying the weapons with him. It wasn't enough. "What if an entire gang ambushes me?"

At forty, Rudy is still afraid to live in a building that doesn't have a doorman, even when that building is in the safest part of town.

In his childhood, Rudy came to a conclusion: he would always be at risk unless he did something about it.

So Rudy came up with a solution. His solution was that he needed to get bigger.

Rudy achieved his solution. He built up lots of muscle.

He even added more solutions. He learned how to fight and use weapons.

How come none of Rudy's solutions worked?

They didn't work because Rudy started with the wrong conclusion. He thought his fear came from being physically unsafe even though he never had any physical risk beyond what most children encounter.

Since Rudy's physical safety was never an issue, he was solving an irrelevant problem. All of Rudy's assaults came from inside of himself. Muscles, fighting, and weapons were never the solution.

We spend our lives self-treating misdiagnosed problems that might have never existed or no longer exist in pursuit of solutions that never mattered in the first place.

Rudy chose muscles. Some people choose money. Other people choose status, career, whom they marry, where they live, etc.

The result is the same even when it looks like they attained what they sought. They're still not happy.

It comes down to this: If you are past your early twenties and you're still not happy, you are probably driven by the wrong conclusions that grew out of faulty or incomplete childhood observations.

Our internal wounds are never addressed by external solutions. If you don't address the internal wounds, your life is being run by the observations, conclusions, and solutions of a five-year-old.

If you cut yourself, you can treat yourself. Except when the cut is deep. If that's the case, you should get treatment. It's a prudent course of action for any wound, emotional or physical.

If you are deeply wounded, seek appropriate treatment. There's no shame in that.

What self-diagnosed childhood problems are you still trying to solve?

_____

What problems did other people claim you had?

_____

What solutions (self-diagnoses) are you still pursuing?

_____

Which ones require treatment from someone other than yourself?

_____

**Work on the problems you really have
and not the ones you self-diagnosed during childhood.**

Paranoid?

Chris and Sergio were at the hardware store to buy some equipment. As Chris walked near a paint display, Sergio got the feeling that one of the cans was going to fall. Should he have said something?

Before you answer, let's add a little more detail. Sergio was a little gun-shy from an accident he had at the same hardware store. But he was certain that he was right about the paint. So should he have said something?

He decided to speak up...

> "Hey, dude," Sergio warned. "Watch out for those paint cans."

> "No worries," Chris replied. "They look fine to me."

> "Are you sure? They look shaky."

> "I hear ya," Chris acknowledged, giving the display a second look. "It's all good."

Chris turned out to be right. Nothing fell. Should he have been pissed at Sergio?

Probably not. Chris knew what was up. He understood that Sergio had recently been conked on the head.

Sergio had done his best with the perspective that he had. He thought something bad might happen, so he said something.

Biased by his own mishap, Sergio voiced his concern. And he was wrong. But that doesn't mean that Chris shouldn't have paid more attention. And it certainly doesn't mean that Sergio had any malice toward Chris. Sergio was just wrong.

What if it's the same way with your paranoid thoughts? What if they are simply reflecting some biased concerns with no more credibility than Sergio had at the hardware store?

Just because those voices say something and just because they're wrong doesn't mean they're out to get you any more than Sergio was out to get Chris.

Wouldn't it be wild if those thoughts were on your side? Even in cases where it does not appear as if they started that way. Even if they're usually not right.

Chris had no problem weighing Sergio's concern. He heard it. He double-checked. He continued walking. After all, better safe than sorry.

What if you could do that with the thoughts inside your head?

What if you could hear your own points of view without bias?

What if you could hear other people's points of view in the same way?

What if your paranoia was treated as a possibility and not an inevitability?

What paranoid concerns do you carry from your childhood?

_____

Have they ever been correct?

_____

If you were able to hear them and quickly move on, would they be a problem?

_____

Treat your thoughts as possibilities instead of inevitabilities.

Terrified?

Brandon and Anthony were talking about how they should allocate funds for a business they were starting...

> "We need to upgrade the fire sprinklers," Brandon proposed.

> "Are you crazy, Brandon? We don't have that kind of money."

> "We can't afford not to," Brandon defended. "Fires are dangerous."

> "Yes, I understand that," Anthony confirmed. "But that's crazy."

> "Listen, I know what it's like. You know I do!"

Their meeting continued on the same course. Brandon made suggestions for safety equipment. Anthony dismissed them. The more Brandon yelled, the faster Anthony tried to shut him down.

Anthony failed to take something essential into account. And he knew better. He and Brandon had grown up together.

Brandon tried to bring it up. He always tried to bring it up. And Anthony always wanted to ignore it. He wanted to ignore the fact that Brandon's house had burned down when he was eight. Brandon couldn't ignore or forget it. He and his family lived in a trailer for nine months.

For obvious reasons, Brandon was terrified about building safety. Given Brandon's history and given that every one of his safety suggestions was shot down, can you imagine what he was thinking?

"Wait until there's a fire. Then he'll see."

The same is true for your terrifying thoughts. The more often they're right, the more trouble you have ignoring them.

While you might think that you don't want those thoughts to come true, a part of you has spent considerable energy sustaining those thoughts and perspectives. That part of you has an investment in being right. If it didn't, you would have been able to drop those perspectives, and you would never be hearing those terrifying thoughts.

But you do hear them because the thoughts are self-sustaining. Nothing sustains them better than being right. And when they're right, you have the perfect self-fulfilling prophecy.

When they're not right, you just figure you lucked out, or you hope the tides have changed. Either way, you're plagued by them.

They're not the same as the casual thoughts you have during the day, like "That flower is pretty." They have much more weight than that.

You likely think that the more you acknowledge a terrifying thought, the more chance of it coming true. So you try to suppress the thoughts that bother you. Even pretend they don't exist.

It's the other way around. The more you attempt to ignore something unpleasant, the more likely it will come true. Why? Because you have to be aware of something in order to suppress it. So the more you suppress an unpleasant possibility, the more it's on your mind.

Acknowledge that you have been terrified by your past. Then notice the difference between then and now.

What thoughts terrify you?

_____

What are they trying to protect you from?

_____

What can you do to satisfy the concern while still moving forward?

_____

Instead of suppressing your older and/or disturbing thoughts, turn up the volume on the others.

Ambiguous?

It was my first time meeting Mac, a tall soft-spoken scientist and truly a sweet guy.

"Why are you here?" I began.

Mac timidly answered in a strangely ethereal and conceptual manner. For instance, he told me...

"I want relationship."

He didn't say "a relationship". Just "I want relationship".

When Mac described things that upset him, he didn't say *he* was upset. Instead, he said...

"I have sadness around that."

I interrupted...

"Mac, do you know that there's no 'there there'? That you're speaking jargon? Where's the 'you' in this?"

Mac didn't know how to respond. In many ways, he was anonymous in his own life.

So I pointed my finger to the floor. With a sweeping motion of my arm, I then pointed to the opposite corner of the room while declaring...

"I want this ball over there! There's no ambiguity. I want this ball over there."

Mac's eyes followed the imaginary ball. I added...

"Do you see how clear that is?

"There's a *me* and there's my objective.

"I might not be right about what I want, but at least I'm not ambiguous.

"Not only that, but by being so clear, you now know enough to assist me if you care to.

"What if I say, 'I want this ball over there, but I don't know how to hit the ball'?

"If there are other people around, someone — hopefully a person who's great at hitting balls — will offer to assist me.

"And I have made it easier for him or her. I didn't waste time. I announced my want. I wasn't wishy-washy.

"Just as important, I told the truth about my abilities. I don't know how to hit the ball. So now someone who likes helping beginners might step up.

"If I *did* know how to hit the ball, but was still having some problems, a more advanced coach might offer assistance."

By this point, Mac had broken into a sweat. It takes commitment to make decisive statements when you have gotten in the habit of being passive. It's a courageous act to make that commitment.

Mac was up for the challenge, so I asked him to start over. There was a night and day difference. His voice, both figuratively and literally, became more powerful.

It was clear that it wasn't a onetime phenomenon. Mac was the sort of person who practiced his sport between lessons. Most don't want to do that. They tell everyone that they're taking lessons. They attend them... sometimes. They do nothing between the lessons. And then they blame their lack of progress on the coach.

The same is true for many people's pursuit of other advice coming from self-help books or anyplace else.

If you don't know where you should be headed — if you are at all ambiguous — then you should be asking for advice on choosing a direction. Otherwise, you will keep ending up in the same state. A state of disappointment.

As obvious as it might sound, once you know where you're headed, in order for someone to give you proper directions, they need to know where you'd like to go *and* the truth about where you currently are. Otherwise, if you are ambiguous or dishonest, the directions won't help.

And of course, after you receive the directions, you need to follow them and make some headway on your own. Otherwise, you'll never get to where you said you wanted to go. You'll waste your time and that of the people who are trying to assist you.

Are you ambiguous about what you want or how to get it?

_____

If you are uncertain, what are you doing to find out?

_____

**Practice clearly stating what you want.
It's okay to start small and work your way up.**

37

Avoiding?

Justin's bookkeeper left a voice mail to remind him about sending her his receipts. It was the end of the year, and she wanted everything to be ready for the accountant. Justin never returned her call.

At the beginning of January, Justin's accountant sent him an e-mail reminder about setting aside some time to get started on his taxes. He wanted to make sure he could fit Justin in. Justin never responded.

In March, Justin's accountant had his assistant call Justin. His schedule was getting tight toward the end of tax season, and he didn't want to be rushed. Justin didn't call back.

Toward the middle of summer, the IRS sent Justin a letter about his delinquent taxes. Justin didn't want to deal with it.

By the following year, the IRS had assessed significant penalties and interest charges. Justin was overwhelmed and didn't have the money to pay.

The cycle repeated itself a couple of times. Justin got further and further behind. Eventually, the IRS seized his assets.

The biggest irony is that Justin had the necessary receipts. He had the money to pay his bookkeeper and accountant. And he had the money to pay his original tax obligation. But he didn't have the funds to cover the penalties, interest charges, and extra accounting expenses that his avoidance caused.

An ignored reminder turned into a warning. An ignored warning turned into an avoidable disaster. It's no different with your thoughts.

In recent studies, it was discovered that the majority of people getting divorces, especially the women, originally had doubts about getting married to their spouses. They avoided those thoughts and got married anyhow.

This is not to say that your negative thoughts are necessarily correct. Only that ignoring them ensures their prophecies.

No different from crossing a street, if you are willing to consider what you fear (such as getting hit by a car), you can take any necessary precautions (such as looking both ways before you cross).

What thoughts have you been avoiding?

_____

What consequences have you faced as a result of avoiding them?

_____

Ask yourself, what feels better between facing your fears head-on or being chased from behind?

Self-Loathing?

Cedric smiles easily. He's a nice guy. On the surface, calm and kind. But there's something underneath the surface. Something people might not notice at first or, in most circumstances, ever observe.

Cedric spent his youth having fistfights. He fought virtually every day. Although a lot more settled than he was in his youth, if someone physically challenges Cedric, there's hell to pay.

And it's fast. Cedric can go from being calm to landing a punch in a blink of an eye. As he explains it, the winner of a fight is the person who gets insane the fastest. And Cedric has no trouble getting insane fast.

Disturbing, isn't it? Why would anyone as calm and kind as Cedric carry such rage? It's crazy. Clearly, this is the perfect argument for why someone should purge their old way of thinking.

But before settling on that assessment about Cedric and his thoughts, consider three more pieces of information...

First of all, when Cedric was a kid, he was beaten so severely that he was literally knocked through walls.

Second, a half-dozen kids in the neighborhood in which Cedric grew up ended up in prison. And two were executed.

Lastly, Cedric is not out of control. Unlike the father who beat him, Cedric was never violent without provocation.

Cedric's thoughts tell him to not let his guard down. To be careful and cautious. To stand up for himself and for others at any cost. Those thoughts and internal voices are the same ones that saved his life.

What do you think now? If it were possible, should Cedric erase those thoughts? If you were walking with Cedric when a mugger attacked, would you not appreciate his abilities?

What makes it work for Cedric? Knowing the difference between then and now. Cedric knows that he no longer lives in the same violent neighborhood in which he grew up. He recognizes that he's no longer surrounded by violence while also knowing that violence does exist. And he's not fighting old demons.

Whether there is a perspective that is keeping you violent or one that is keeping you timid, it is there for a reason.

Whether there is a voice you hear that keeps you shy or one that tempts you to be obnoxious, it's there for a reason.

Those thoughts and behaviors are not there by accident. They might have protected you from something. Maybe even from someone. For that they should be appreciated.

In the majority of cases, all of our attributes are useful. Even the inconvenient ones. What makes the inconvenient ones inconvenient is using them at the wrong time.

If Cedric got violent during a normal conversation, that would be the wrong time. But as previously mentioned, if he got violent when legitimately threatened or when someone he cared about was in danger, then that would be useful.

It's useful when marine drill instructors yell at recruits to mold them into soldiers. It's not so beneficial when they're yelling at their kids.

It's useful to defer to someone who knows more than you. It's not so useful when you are the leader and people are looking to you for direction.

In all cases, you want the right behaviors at the right time, even for ones you wouldn't expect to be useful. For example...

We could dismiss dissatisfaction as bad behavior, worthy of jettisoning. And yes, dissatisfaction can be a problem. On the other hand, dissatisfaction is likely the initial inspiration behind all inventions and accomplishments.

If an inventor was satisfied with how things were, there would be no motivation to create something new. In this way, dissatisfaction becomes a motivation to get started. But after you're on your way, dissatisfaction will slow you down. So you switch to inspiration, education, and so on for the rest of the journey.

The secret is using the right behaviors at the right time and combining them with other appropriate behaviors and actions.

Even your tentative behaviors, like fear, might give you just enough pause to stop and reconsider. That's a good thing unless you're fearing something from the past and not considering the difference between back then and now.

If you are self-loathing, how about cutting yourself a little slack?

Let's see if there's a way to be appropriate with your thoughts and behaviors instead of hating yourself for having them.

What do you loathe about yourself?

_____

How did this loathsome attribute or thought help keep you alive?

_____

How can you utilize those attributes in the present?

_____

What's the difference between your childhood and now?

_____

**Be thankful for being alive
and thank all of your selves for getting you here.**

Unappreciative?

Bernie was a factory worker who had been with the same company for nearly twenty years. Similar to most of his coworkers, he was dedicated and untiring.

When the company went through hard times, Bernie and his buddies stuck it out, even when the payroll was late.

When the company was having good times, Bernie and his buddies were thrilled, even though the profits never seemed to trickle down to their paychecks.

One day, one of Bernie's coworkers overheard some of the management team talking.

> "The automation initiative is really cool," a guy in a black suit exclaimed.

> "You bet. I can't wait," a gray-suited man agreed.

> "The manufacturing department hasn't announced it yet, has it?"

> "Definitely not," Gray Suit responded. "None of those workers are going to be happy about it. They're all getting laid off."

> "Really?" Black Suit questioned. "Some of them have been here a really long time."

"That's true, but they've outlived their usefulness. We don't need them anymore."

Word of the automation and layoffs spread throughout the company. Within a couple of months, the workers unionized. And a couple of months after that, they went on strike.

Within weeks of the strike, the company's sales and profit plunged. Management pleaded with the workers. They begged them to show the loyalty they were known for.

But the workers wouldn't listen. They had lost all trust in their employer. They were tired of being unappreciated. The time had come for them to watch out for themselves.

The strike eventually ended, but things never returned to the way they were. There was tension in the air. The upper management and workers stopped talking.

The company lost so much money that it couldn't afford the full-blown automation that management had originally envisioned. Besides that, whatever was automated failed because the workers had no incentive to support it. Instead, they had every reason to sabotage it.

If only upper management had not been so quick to abandon the workers to whom the company owed its success. If only the company had offered to update the older workers' skills and retrain them. If only it had shown the workers the appreciation they deserved.

Your childhood thoughts are no different from those workers. As crazy as it might sound, they are akin to living entities. You already feel that way about your most dominant thoughts. The ones you might call "the real you". They're the dominant thoughts you're having this very moment.

The rest of those thoughts are viewed as the bad guys. Not the real you. Your negative voices. Your other side. Your dark side.

Even if those thoughts served some value in the past, you probably think there's no place for them now. You certainly don't appreciate them.

Perhaps you're angry that they are there. Perhaps you think they should have somehow done a better job of protecting you or setting you on the right course.

Regardless of your judgments, they're living entities inside of you. As noted in another chapter, if they weren't living entities, you would have been able to drop them a long time ago. But you can't. They persist whether you like it or not, and whether you like them or not.

As an entity, what would you do if the other entities around you wanted to have you removed? What would you do if people around you said you had outlived your usefulness?

The answer is fairly obvious. If you wanted to live, you would fight for your survival, no different from what the factory workers did. You would sabotage all other efforts, especially those that were plotting your demise.

Does a legitimately formed thought and perspective, one that has kept you alive, deserve your disdain and/or lack of appreciation? Does it deserve your attempts to kill it?

If one part of you is able to turn against another...

If you can justify the disregard and lack of appreciation because its usefulness has passed or it has gotten inconvenient or you never liked it in the first place...

...then how stable do you think you can ever be inside of yourself?

How could you ever achieve harmony? How about a sense of calm?

Doesn't it make sense to retrain those thoughts? To update their context to the present?

Doesn't it make sense to show all of you some appreciation?

Besides, who the hell are you to determine what part of you should be appreciated and which part should not?

What parts of yourself do you not appreciate?

_____

What negative traits are you trying to abandon?

_____

What could you do to make those parts of yourself more up-to-date and relevant?

_____

Remember that no part of you is disposable.

Revising?

Mustik & Sons had been a family-run business for sixty-five years when the patriarchs, Bert and Francis, passed away.

Their three children stepped in to run the company. Each of the kids had spent some portion of their childhood working there, but none of them liked it. They wanted nothing to do with an old manufacturing company. It was a dirty blue-collar vestige of the past.

From the children's perspective, the family business had always been an embarrassment. Something they had to hide. But at the same time, it was something they couldn't escape. They resented the fact that it was their source of money. And they cringed at their parents' disregard for appearances.

The children always wished that Bert and Francis had been better educated like their friends' parents were. After all, their friends' parents were business executives and intellectuals. They drove fancier cars, took their kids on luxury vacations, and had manicured fingernails unsullied from factory soot.

Whereas Bert and Francis prided themselves on creating a family of employees, their children wanted none of that. They resented the familiarity everyone had with them. From the kids' way of thinking, it was too presumptuous. They weren't the same children the workers saw growing up. They were new people. Adults. Different. Better than their past.

Gone were the company picnics, Christmas parties, and birthday celebrations. Company focus turned solely to profit and a new vision. No more manufacturing. Mustik & Sons would transform itself into an "information services" company. And it certainly wouldn't be called Mustik & Sons. Too stodgy. Too linked to the past.

Manufacturing continued only long enough to finance its own demise. Within two years, the transformation was complete. The entire facility received a face-lift. The factory equipment was removed just like the workers that had been there for generations.

After two years and seven weeks, something went horribly wrong. The new mainframe computers overtaxed the old infrastructure. In order to effect repairs, wiring and other utilities needed to be located beneath the solid concrete floor of the old factory building.

But none of the new workers knew where to find them. They didn't even know where the building plans were located. The Mustik heirs were desperate. So they tracked down Abe, one of the former factory foremen, for assistance.

Not surprisingly, Abe wasn't inclined to help. He especially resented the implied expectation that he owed his former employer. If those "Mustik brats" needed his assistance, they'd have to pay through the nose: $50,000 in cash, to be exact.

The brats agreed. They had no other choice.

When Abe showed up at the then-unrecognizable headquarters of what used to be Mustik & Sons, he was carrying a tool bag in his right hand. He ignored the insincere and resentful attitudes of the people perfunctorily greeting him. He just held out his left hand and waited for his $50,000.

After having the cash spitefully slapped into his palm, Abe counted the bills and dropped them into one of the compartments of the tool bag. Then he calmly walked to what used to be one of the factory floors. It was now a room filled with fancy cubicles and gray carpet. Elevator music had replaced the cacophony of the old equipment.

Ignoring all of the suit-wearing employees who judgmentally stared at him with the same disdain they had for their janitors, Abe found the spot he was looking for, knelt down, pulled a can of spray paint out of his bag, and sprayed a red *X* onto the brand-new carpet.

> "There ya go," Abe announced.
>
> "That's it?" one of the heirs challenged. "$50,000 f——ing dollars for you to paint a damn red *X* on the floor?"
>
> "Nope," Abe replied. "$50,000 f——ing dollars for knowing where to paint the damn red *X* on the floor."

Even if you did not recognize that old joke, perhaps you will recognize Oscar Wilde...

> "To regret one's own experiences is to arrest one's own development. To deny one's own experiences is to put a lie into the lips of one's own life. It is no less than a denial of the soul."

What about yourself have you tried to deny, hide, and/or revise?

_____

What beneficial experiences does your past provide?

_____

How can you utilize them to move forward?

_____

Consider the wisdom of Shakespeare's King Henry VI:

**"Let me embrace thee, sour adversity,
for wise men say it is the wisest course."**

Foreboding?

Leila was married to an extremely handsome man. Franklin was a six-foot-one fashion model who was on numerous fashion and fitness magazine covers, as well as those of romance novels. Most did not think that Leila was nearly as attractive as Franklin. She certainly did not think she was.

In the fifteen and sixteen hundreds, Leila would have been referred to as Rubenesque. She couldn't understand why Franklin married her. Every time Leila looked at magazines featuring her husband's physique, she recognized the obvious contrast between her plump frame and the thinness of Franklin's female counterparts.

Leila lived in constant agony. She was jealous of everyone, man or woman, with whom Franklin spent time. If Franklin was talking to a neighbor outside, Leila would hide behind the drapes and peer out. She was never comfortable leaving him alone in public. What if a more attractive woman or even man lured him away?

Leila always wanted to know where Franklin was, what he was doing, to whom he was talking, and when he would be back. She was certain that Franklin would leave her.

Despite all of Leila's surveillance, there was one thing she somehow failed to observe. It was obvious to anyone who saw Franklin and Leila together. Plain as day.

Franklin was madly in love with Leila. His eyes sparkled and teared whenever he talked about her. In his mind and heart, Leila was the perfect woman. His dream come true. From the time he met her, he never looked at another woman.

Leila and Franklin divorced after one year of marriage. Franklin eventually chose someone else. But not for the reasons Leila imagined.

Franklin left Leila because she repelled him. He was in love with her. He wanted to be with her. But he eventually could not contend with Leila's foreboding thoughts.

When they first met, Franklin told Leila that she was the only woman he ever loved. That wasn't enough.

He asked her to marry him. That wasn't enough.

He wrote her poetry. That wasn't enough.

He begged her to go to couples counseling. That wasn't enough.

Franklin was sobbing during their final therapy session. Barely able to speak the words, he told Leila that he had run out of things he could try. He had attempted everything to have her believe him.

When Franklin finished speaking, Leila silently stared at him for several seconds. Finally, she turned to their therapist and said...

"I *knew* it. I always knew he'd leave me."

Case closed. Leila had all of the proof she needed. She was right. Her prophecy came true.

Almost.

What really came true was Leila's self-fulfilling prophecy. Of course, there was a chance that her marriage would end. That's a possibility in all marriages. On its own, it was but a single possibility. But Leila treated it as an inevitability. She consciously and unconsciously ensured the outcome.

Your foreboding thoughts are merely recipes.

They're not at all dangerous on the cookbook page.

But if you insist on mixing the ingredients, you'll bake disaster.

What are your foreboding thoughts?

_____

What have you ignored and/or continue to ignore in order to make them come true?

_____

Choose happiness over righteousness.

Squandering?

Zander, for the most part, is happy. Blake, for the most part, is not.

Zander plays life like a sport — he is always striving to be better. Blake plays life like a contest — he just wants to score.

Zander painstakingly works to improve himself. Blake opportunistically seeks fortuity.

Zander's response to any observation and correction is always inquiry ("Please tell me more!"). Blake's response is always denial ("I don't do that!").

Since Zander is looking to explore, he always has traction to move forward. Since Blake chooses to deny, he always gets nowhere.

People love helping Zander because he effectively implements their suggestions. People hate assisting Blake because he won't do the work.

When something doesn't go well for Zander, he looks to see what he could have done differently. When things don't work out for Blake, he points out what everyone *else* should have done differently.

Zander confronts his deepest demons and cries. Blake blames his demons and whines.

They both had horrible childhoods. Zander forgave but didn't forget. He moved forward and built loving relationships with his family. Blake continues to complain. His family relationships remain stuck in the past.

Zander's children have a father who sees them. Blake's children have a father who sees only himself.

All of Zander's losses teach him lessons. All of Blake's losses teach him nothing.

At Zander's worst, he has pain without regret. At Blake's best, he has sorry excuses for getting nowhere.

Zander tells the truth about his potential. Blake fantasizes some greater destiny.

Zander has led a full life and will continue with great prospect. Blake has only what remains of his life and had better get started living it.

Zander loves hearing reality because he harnesses it. If Blake accepted reality, he would realize he squandered his life.

What have you been squandering?

_____

What blessings?

_____

Which attributes?

_____

Whose assistance?

_____

What possibilities?

_____

Choose responsibility over blame.

Entitled?

Paul is your run-of-the-mill guy. He's not flashy, overimposing, mean, or offensive in any way. He's just a nice guy who owes Sandy money.

"Hey, Paul," Sandy asked, "where is it?"

"Where's what?"

"The money," Sandy clarified. "The money you promised to pay me."

"Oh jeez, Sandy, I don't have it."

"Why not? You said you'd have it by the end of the week. Why are you making me work so hard when I'm the one doing you a favor?"

"I know," Paul halfheartedly admitted. "I'll get it to you next week."

"This is the third time you told me that," Sandy protested. "I don't know what to do. You said you needed money, so I lent it to you. You keep saying you'll pay me back, but you don't. Meanwhile, you go out to dinner with your friends, go to the movies, and who knows what."

"But —"

> "I don't want to hear it, Paul. Why do you keep
> making me responsible for your problems?"

We tend to believe that entitled people are obnoxious. Or we see them as those who think too highly of themselves. That might be true. That behavior is certainly in the wheelhouse of an entitled person. But that's not what's at the heart of entitlement.

The opposite of "responsible" is not just "irresponsible". The opposite is also "entitled". To whatever degree you don't take responsibility for getting what you want and delivering what you promised, you're being entitled. It's as simple as that.

If you are lamenting a situation and doing nothing to improve it, you're acting entitled.

If people are counting on you for the most minor of things to the most important and you are not delivering, you're being entitled.

If you are burdening other people with your problems and are not putting in more effort to fix them than they are, then you're being entitled. This is true even if you are sick and are not doing your best to get better, not doing whatever you can within your limitations, or not profusely appreciating the people who have and are helping you.

If you are thinking things should be different and aren't doing anything about it, you're acting entitled.

If you are behaving as if everything is fine while causing someone else worry, you're being entitled.

If you are complaining about things and not coming up with and pursuing solutions, you're being entitled.

Entitlement applies to the biggest and smallest aspects of life. If you are rude to people, just talk about yourself, don't acknowledge others, don't pull your car over when you hear sirens or when other drivers are trying to get past you, turn without signaling, take two parking spaces, park illegally, chat during movies, talk loudly on your phone in public, wear too much perfume, leave unwanted groceries items anywhere in the store other than where they belong, litter, don't bus your tray at fast-food restaurants, undertip for good service and/or expect tips for bad service, overcharge for your work product, keep people waiting, don't show up when promised, cheat in games or in relationships, fib or lie for your own benefit, requisition office supplies, steal, buy products you can't afford, unnecessarily put yourself at risk, scare people, have children you knowingly cannot support, consider yourself more important than society or your wants more essential than the greater good, or bestow other liberties upon yourself, then you're being entitled.

Oops. Did you just see yourself in that list? I did. I have zoomed through my share of yellow lights and coasted through rolling stops, not to mention walked my dogs without a leash.

The fact is that we're all entitled to some degree, and we typically rationalize our way through the perpetrations.

> "Just this once."

> "I'm in a hurry."

> "No one was around."

> "Well, at least I didn't ——."

But it's all entitlement.

In the very first chapter, I mentioned...

> "If you want to get some value from this book,
> make it your job to see how you are similar to

every single person. How you can feel what they must be feeling. How you can understand why they have done what they have done. See what you do that's similar, even if it's not identical."

That message certainly applies to entitlement. We all have some of it in us.

Consider a colander. No matter how much liquid gets added. No matter how hot. No matter how cold. No matter how thick. No matter how thin. Colanders always drain.

It has little to do with the content and everything to do with the vessel.

The more holes, the faster it drains.

The more holes located at the bottom, the more likely it drains to emptiness.

The emptier we are, the less happy we are.

It's as simple as that.

What do you think you're entitled to?

_____

How do you know it's true?

_____

Have you noticed that your satisfaction doesn't last?

_____

Match your efforts to your desires.
Know the difference between wishing and working.
And don't presume to have rights you don't really have.

Complaining?

Sarah had a daily complaint. Her work commute took too long. When asked about her route, she lamented taking the freeway. When I suggested side streets, she rolled her eyes.

> "That's crazy," she complained. "Everyone knows the freeway is faster."

> "Great, you know best," I replied. "Enjoy the drive."

The following week, Sarah was still complaining about her commute. Having my advice dismissed, there wasn't much I could recommend.

> "Either get some audio books, make some calls, or try a different route."

What else could I say?

As if she were doing me a favor, Sarah claimed she would try a surface street and, the following week, was happy to let me know that I was wrong. It had taken her twice as long.

> "That's great news," I replied. "Now you have more appreciation for the freeway. And by the way, did you see any other streets along the way?"

By repeating the same behavior, all Sarah did was complain. By trying something different, she could see whether her complaint was reasonable.

If she would have explored further, Sarah might have discovered some different side streets or maybe even a combination of surface streets and the freeway.

Or she could have explored other times.

Or she could have moved.

Or she could have changed jobs.

Or she could have telecommuted.

Or she could have gotten used to the drive.

Or, as I said earlier, she could have made some phone calls or enjoyed some audio books.

Our persistent dissatisfactions are no accident. They come from commitment. Commitment to a point of view. Commitment to having a complaint.

If you are stuck to a point of view, you'll be stuck in life.

If you do nothing more than complain, not only will you be stuck, but you will also be suffering. And so will everyone around you.

What are the top three things you always complain about?

_____

What other possibilities should you be considering?

_____

Choose resolving over whining.

Backward?

The ice cream shop's tables were filled with patrons enjoying their frozen delights.

In contrast, completely absent of delight, was a visibly angry ice cream server scowling over the counter like a prisoner behind bars.

Equally noticeable was his empty tip jar. Not a single patron had seen fit to make a contribution, save four pennies and a nickel.

The reason was obvious. The employee's demeanor was as cold as the ice cream.

I attempted to break through with a smile and pleasant greeting. He was having none of it. His only focus, while trying to stare through me, was the empty jar.

Dismissing my best efforts, he begrudgingly shoved my ice cream cone toward me as he looked at the jar. It wasn't as if I was being begged or even reminded to tip him. It was as if I was being dared not to.

So I did what most of the other patrons apparently did. I put my change in my pocket and walked away from the counter.

If I had asked Grumpy to tell me what was wrong and if he would have deemed my question worthy of answering, he would have likely groused that he was pissed about not receiving any tips. He would have told me that it was always that way and that people were such jerks. And he might have promised a better attitude had he only received some financial love.

In Grumpy's mind, everyone else needed to go first. We were supposed to reward him, and then he would give us something to reward.

Of course, that's backward. If he did not behave like a jerk, most of the world wouldn't treat him as one.

As I was driving home, I noticed a sticker and license plate frame on a minivan ahead of me. Since we were stopped at a light, I even took a picture.

The sticker said...

"Don't talk to me, asshole."

And the license frame read...

"I see dumb people."

I imagine this guy never receives the benefit of a friendly police officer cutting him some slack. Instead, he spends his days being treated as he consistently predicts.

But obviously, the treatment he receives is not a confirmation of any prophetic abilities. It's not a prediction at all. It's a setup. A near certainty. No different from the ice cream server's.

Despite the likelihood that both of these people see themselves as edgy or daring, at some point, they both stopped taking risks. Rather than chancing the fear of being treated unkindly, they decided it was better to "predict" and succumb to their foretold fate rather than being unpleasantly surprised.

Their behavior gives them the illusion that they're making a choice. They lead with rudeness and tell themselves it's why the world is mean back. It's all pretend.

They have convinced themselves that the rest of us in the world are at fault. Ice Cream Guy might smile if we only gave him tips. And Minivan Man might remove his bumper sticker and license plate frame if intelligent people would talk to him and everyone was nice.

It's backward.

This book's message is fairly obvious if not redundant...

> First: When it comes to your past, what you think is isn't.

> Second: You would do better appreciating yourself for who you are instead of who you wish yourself to be.

If you are like most people being given this information, you might be promising to appreciate yourself as soon as ———.

If you could just get rid of that one little thing, perhaps reduced down from a dozen previous complaints, then you could love yourself.

Then everything will be fine.

It won't because it's backward.

There can't be conditions.

Love yourself first and watch what happens.

Instead of backwardly withholding your love until your provisos are met, is it possible that you could love yourself unconditionally?

Are you willing to try?

Never use your love as a bargaining chip against yourself or others.

Resigned?

"Mom, when are we leaving?" Jackson pleaded. "We've been here FOREVER!"

"Pretty soon," Jackson's mom replied.

"We're NEVER never going to leave," Jackson whined.

That's exactly how most people feel about their lives. We feel as if our pain will last forever and that a resolution will never arrive.

On the previous pages, I illustrated examples of uninformed observations, faulty conclusions, and misguided solutions. They're easy to see in other people and not so easy to recognize in ourselves.

We might be able to change our thoughts if we intellectually realize other possibilities, but our feelings are still another matter. For example...

Think about going to someone's house for dinner. You have arrived on time, and you're starving, especially because you skipped lunch in anticipation of enjoying a great meal.

But dinner isn't ready. Your host apologizes and explains that she had oven problems. So you're not worried. Everything is solved, and dinner is just thirty minutes from completion.

It's a reasonable explanation. You completely understand. So are you still hungry? Of course you are.

Our intellectual realizations don't change our physical sensations. Likewise, they often cannot change our emotional ones either.

Dinner is thirty long minutes away. How long does it feel to a kid? To a five-year-old? It feels like forever. When will dinner be served? Feels like never.

Children have little or no sense of time. Is it any wonder that the awful things we experience when we are young seem to last forever? So is it surprising that our predictions for when it will be better are "never"?

In our young minds, we will always be lonely. We will always be afraid. We will always be sad.

We start with observations.

> "Daddy is mad."

> "Daddy is always mad."

Then we have conclusions.

> "I'm bad."

> "I deserve to be punished."

> "I don't deserve to be happy."

> "I will never be happy."

And then we attempt to solve the problem.

> "I'm going to be the best girl ever."

"I'm going to make people love me."

or...

"Screw it. Screw them. I'm just going to take care of myself."

Sometimes we are aware of our observations and conclusions. Sometimes not.

Sometimes we are intellectually hopeful, but emotionally resigned.

Sometimes we use positive thinking in an attempt to overcome our deeply rooted resignation.

And we long for explanations and epiphanies.

It doesn't matter because, just like with hunger, intellectual realizations don't change the pangs.

Any positive thinking aside, what have you resigned yourself into believing is unrecoverable and/or unsolvable?

_____

What did you vow to change about yourself?

_____

What feeling seems to have been with you forever?

_____

What are you afraid might never change?

_____

**Make peace with who you are.
Then work with what you have.**

Unsophisticated?

A child's equation for escaping pain:
THIS + THAT = HAPPINESS

It's a fairly unsophisticated formula, but what can you expect from a child?

More sophisticated formulas include more advanced functions. Most importantly, they include the concept of "conditions", as in:

> If this person is around, then:
> > I feel bad about myself.

> If they're not around, then:
> > I feel great.

Conditions take other people and context into consideration, which is something we are unable to do when we are younger. By their very definition, children are egocentric. So as children, we only see ourselves in the equation.

As unsophisticated as they might be, we hope that our childhood equations, our strategies, will help us avoid our fears.

It becomes more than a hope; it becomes an obsession. We remain hypervigilant and always tracking.

Have you ever driven on a windy mountain road? Do you know what happens when someone is excessively worried about heading over the embankment? They head right toward it.

Just like driving on a mountain road, our desperation to avoid the painful conclusions we reached in our childhood leads us toward them.

We might think we know better and that making the same mistakes is impossible, yet we prove otherwise nearly every day.

What unsophisticated formulas are you still using?

_____

What mistakes do you keep repeating?

_____

What five things are different between now and when you were a child?

_____

Give up the notion that any single event or accomplishment leads to lifelong happiness.

Wrong?

Neal was having a conversation with one of his closest friends whom he rarely saw. Caleb lived out of the country, so whenever he and Neal got together, they would start by sharing the three most significant events that happened to each of them since they had last seen each other.

> "Wow," Caleb said after Neal finished sharing his stories, "all of those illustrate the same lesson."

> "No, they don't," Neal denied.

> "Yes, they DO," Caleb laughed.

In the middle of denying Caleb's observation, Neal had a second of thought that seemed to go on for minutes.

> "I wonder if Caleb is right," Neal said to himself.
> "Yep, I think he might be right... Damn, he's
> definitely right... Hmmm, am I going to admit it?"

Neal sat silently, for what seemed like an eternity, before he blurted....

> "Yeah, you're right."

Caleb held his stomach from laughing so hard. He, of course, already knew that he was right. It was only Neal who had been claiming otherwise.

Neal thought it over the next day. He had been sitting with one of his closest friends.

They loved each other.

They were safe in each other's company.

Neither was looking to hurt the other.

They were alone, so there was no risk of embarrassment.

And they were talking about something that didn't have much significance.

Yet, despite all that, Neal felt compelled to be right.

> "Jeez," he thought to himself, "if I'm that driven to be right in the most ideal of circumstances, what must I be like when the situation doesn't feel as safe?"

It's a sobering thought for us all. How much energy do we devote to defending our point of view?

How much greater is our defense when we think our point of view is significant, even sacred? Like the conclusions we reached when we were children.

How much more entrenched do we get for every year our point of view has been with us?

In continued contemplation, Neal realized something else. He had been so busy resisting Caleb's observation that he couldn't remember the point Caleb was trying to convey.

In our preoccupation to be right, we miss so much.

What are the things you think you need to be right about?

_____

What topics are people not allowed to discuss with you?

_____

What are the points you keep ignoring?

_____

**Opt for knowledge over pride
and discovery over dogma.**

Needy?

"Mom, can I have an ice cream cone?"

"No, you may not."

"But, Mooooommmmm, I need it!"

Early in our lives, we learn the power of the word "need". We think of it like an industrial-strength "want".

We use our self-declared needs to keep our childhood conclusions and strategies in play. We don't just want to be popular; we need it. We don't just want people to like us; we need them to adore us.

If we don't get what we want, it's a pisser. But if we don't get what we need, it's a tragedy. So as soon as we declare something to be a need, the stakes go up.

As humans, we only have five legitimate needs: air, food, shelter, water, and companionship. The prospect of not getting what we need leads us to desperation.

For the list of five, that's reasonable. Getting desperate when your air supply gets cut off is understandable. Most everything else we desire is not in the same league.

Neediness also tires people out. Ever see the husband of someone who needs to look young, beautiful, and/or rich? He looks like the life has been sucked out of him. Such is the case whenever interacting with a needy person. It's grueling.

Neediness can never be satisfied. If someone gives us something because we falsely claimed a need, it feels obligatory. Something only feels heartfelt when it is given in response to a legitimate need or want.

If we mislabel our wants as needs, we guarantee a self-fulfilling prophecy of never feeling as if someone truly cares.

Need what you need.

Want what you want.

And don't get the two confused.

What wants have you mislabeled as needs?

_____

What can you never get enough of?

_____

What do you fear not having?

_____

Notice you have what you need.
Then have fun getting what you want.

Desperate?

Ty was eating at a local pizzeria when he suddenly began to gasp for air. His eyes watered and bulged as he tried to catch his breath.

Fortunately, an ambulance crew was dining at the same restaurant. In record time, they ran to their vehicle, grabbed an oxygen tank, rushed back, and strapped the mask over Ty's mouth.

Just as a paramedic reached to turn the valve, Ty shakily held up a hand in objection while using his other to pull off the mask.

"No!" Ty gasped with his final breath of air.

"Why not?" the EMT shouted.

"I don't like that brand of oxygen."

What? You don't believe my story? Why is that?

Is it because you know that when someone is desperate, they don't have the benefit of choices — that they, instead, are compelled to take whatever is offered?

If that's what you think, you're right. The problem with desperation is that it leaves us without a full range of choices. At best, it's like the pressure we feel when forced to answer a multiple-choice test.

It's better to have possibilities. Instead of having a limited set of choices, you can fill in the blanks with whatever you desire.

If you are pursuing a possibility and don't succeed, you can try again or pursue another possibility.

On the other hand, when you pursue something out of desperation and don't succeed, it becomes a tragedy.

"Oh well" versus "Oh no!"

What are you desperate to have?

_____

What fake tragedies do you keep repeating and/or lamenting?

_____

What desires are you embarrassed to express?

_____

Remember to breathe.

Smug?

Ted's father was never all there. He lived in the same house, was at breakfast every morning, and attended the family get-togethers. But there was always a distance that Ted could feel.

Most disturbing was the lack of warmth that Ted noticed between his mother and father. Their relationship felt platonic. Ted declared that he would never be that way when he got married.

When Ted was thirteen, his father left. Turns out that Dad had been having an affair since Ted was two. Ted's mom was devastated. She always felt the existence of the other woman. She just didn't want to think about it. And after her husband left, she never wanted to discuss it.

Ted knew to never bring it up, just as much as he knew he would never be like his dad. He would never inflict the same pain.

Fifteen years later, Ted was married with three kids. Things were great at home and at work. He was pastor of a small congregation and loved it.

As part of his regular duties, Ted counseled parishioners. That was the only part of Ted's life in which he felt troubled. Whenever a congregant discussed having an affair, Ted struggled with forgiveness.

If only they knew how much pain they were causing, they'd surely see the error of their ways and return to their spouses. To Ted, it was as simple as that. Ted was smug in his certainty. He didn't think it was in his nature to be so judgmental, but there was no denying it.

As the economy got worse and Ted found himself working longer hours with the church's loyal volunteers, his home life became strained. His wife began resenting what she thought was Ted's greater devotion to his congregation than to his own family. Ted knew that it was only temporary. His wife didn't understand, but the volunteers did. Especially Susan.

It's pretty obvious where this is going. Ted and Susan had an affair, and Ted grew more distant from his family. Ted followed in his father's footsteps.

How did this happen? Because Ted was smug. He thought it was impossible for him to do what his father did. It was impossible that he would ever be tempted by another woman. It was impossible that he would repeat his childhood circumstances.

And so Ted made a crucial error. Smugness leads to complacency. Because he believed it was impossible to make the same mistakes as his father, he took no precautions. If he would have accepted that he could be overpowered by an attraction to another woman, he could have done a better job of avoiding tempting situations, like working late with a young widow.

As children, we typically know only black and white, good and bad, mean and nice, happy and sad. It's one or the other. As we grow up, we hopefully learn that it's not that simple.

Even if we do learn about complexities, we continue to be driven, even compelled, by the simplistic points of view we developed as children.

There's no sophistication in the thought and no room for adjustment. We must be rich. We must be pretty. We must be popular.

We will never work just for money. We will never be sick. We will never make the same mistakes as our parents.

The more smug we are about something not happening, the more likely it will come to pass.

Smugness is a desperate attempt to mask and deny something we're afraid of.

Where are you smug as in holier-than-thou?

_____

What have you grown up claiming you would never do?

_____

What outcome do you think is impossible?

_____

Whose behavior do you find yourself judging?

_____

Whom should you be talking to about your underlying fear?

_____

**Notice that declaring your fears away hasn't worked.
Face them.**

Denying?

As a slight guy of 140 pounds, with a bad back and a recent disk surgery under his belt, Abe decided that he was going to remodel his house on his own.

Everything was going well until a structural beam needed to be raised. Since Abe didn't have anyone helping him, he tried to lift the beam on his own. Even without back surgery, that wasn't something that Abe should have attempted. It was a reality that Abe denied.

It didn't work out so well with the beam. Abe's back gave out. The beam crashed down. Abe woke up in the hospital and found himself in a wheelchair, just like the one his dad was confined to when Abe was six. To top it off, from that moment on, Abe needed constant care.

When Abe was a child, his father was crippled. Abe was embarrassed by his father's dependence on others. So Abe reached some important decisions in his youth. He would never be needy like his father. He would be the opposite. Abe chose near-total independence as his strategy. And he denied his limitations.

Abe's childhood solution landed him exactly where he didn't want to be. Ironically, while trying to be who he was not (a he-man), Abe inadvertently denied himself the benefit of his actual attributes. For example...

Abe bypassed his ingenuity. He could have used a hoist.

Abe forgot that he had money. He could have hired someone.

Abe ignored the fact that he had time. Moving the beam could have waited.

And Abe missed the fact that he had friends. They all would have been happy to help.

In other words, Abe's attempt to deny his limitations denied him access to his own abilities.

You cannot deny without being denied.

Whenever we pretend to be someone we're not...

Whenever we act as if we have something that we don't...

Whenever we deny others the benefit of being who they are because we're busy acting as if we have their abilities...

We deny ourselves the virtue of who we are...

We deny ourselves the enjoyment of what we already have...

And we deny ourselves the gift of what our friends have to offer.

What limitations do you deny?

_____

What assistance should you be accepting from family and friends?

_____

What assistance should you be providing?

_____

**Choose partnership over isolation
and contribution over stinginess.**

Posing?

> "How do you need to be seen?" I asked Gary. "And
> if you're not seen this way, you're upset."

Gary performed his usual ritual prior to speaking. He looked up
from his notes, pushed his glasses up the bridge of his nose,
cleared his throat, slightly cocked his head to the left, and
declared...

> "Intelligent."

And as he always did at the conclusion of speaking, Gary
thoughtfully nodded his head. He was agreeing with himself and
coaxing anyone around — in this case, me — to agree with him.

Gary was posing as intelligent. When most people look at him,
they would never think, "There's an intelligent guy." If anything,
they would think, "There's someone trying to look intelligent."

Similarly, when we see an older person with too much plastic
surgery, we don't think, "There's someone young." We think,
"There's someone trying to look young." Or at the very best:
"There's someone who looks good for their age." We don't
mistake them as young any more than someone mistaking Gary
for intelligent.

It's no different from people trying to look cool, sexy, athletic,
successful, etc. There are many disguises. Hairstyle and color.

Hip clothing. Tattoos. Jewelry and chains. Glasses. Cars. Etcetera. It's all about posing.

As children, we attempt to solve our feelings of inadequacy by declaring how we need to be seen. Instead of desiring to be seen as we are, we crave to be seen as we wish we were. And then we put together our disguise.

Consider the problem. We need to be seen in a certain way in order to not be upset. We are not that way, so most do not see us as we require. That means we spend our entire lives being upset.

Ironically, in our demands to be seen in a particular way and not succeeding, we actually induce the same feelings of inadequacy we had as children.

If we do succeed in getting people to believe that we are our pretense, we succeed in not being seen for who we really are. And so then again, we induce the same feelings of inadequacy we had as children.

Using the "I won't call you on your BS (your posing) if you don't call me on mine" technique, we find people to lie to us if we're willing to lie to them.

We see that every day in people who fib to one another about how good they look or, at least, leave the obvious unsaid. That works until there's an argument. That's when we hear, "I never thought you were ———."

By posing as intelligent, Gary obscured his real virtues. He discounted himself and his virtues, and others did the same.

The shame in trying to be someone we're not, is that we miss discovering, enjoying, and sharing the wonderful virtues of who we really are.

Even if someone believes our disguise, we still know the truth. And so we live in constant fear of being found out. One part fights to keep the disguise while another feels the loneliness of never truly being seen.

Posers never feel good about themselves.

What do you do in your dress, speech, and presentation to pose as someone other than who you are?

_____

How do you need people to see you?

_____

How do you feel if they don't see you that way?

_____

What are you afraid people might see if you drop the pretense?

_____

Save your costumes for Halloween.

Bitter?

Nancy was certain that she deserved the very best in life. She was entitled to a handsome husband who adored her, lots of money, and everything that she could imagine provided for.

But life had other plans for Nancy. Things were not working out as she had expected. Nancy thought something was definitely wrong. Not with her, but with life itself. As far as Nancy was concerned, God was messing up.

With every utterance of every complaint, Nancy grew more entrenched in her dissatisfaction and more certain of her entitlement. Gentle coaching and helpful suggestions were having no effect, so I needed to be more direct.

> "Nancy, the first thing you need to know," I began, "is that you're standing on the precipice of bitterness. Once you tumble down that cliff, there's no scaling back up.

> "I have never ever seen anyone recover from being bitter. It leaves deep and hardened wrinkles on your face as well as a coldness in your soul."

Needless to say, I got Nancy's attention.

> "Second," I continued, "the proof that you are NOT entitled to what you think you're entitled to is that

> IF you were entitled to it, you would have it by now.
>
> "Life has already responded to the terms you're demanding. It said, 'No!'
>
> "So get over yourself, drop the attitude, and step down from your soapbox."

As advertised, this wasn't subtle, nor was it inaccurate. Nancy really was heading toward bitterness, and there really isn't any way to recover from that. Your only option is to step back before it's too late.

> "I don't get it," Nancy persisted after recovering from her shock. "Just look at me!"
>
> "Yes, you certainly are quite a catch," I agreed. "And people can understand what you want. But here's the thing: You think you're entitled to too much. And your entitlement is repellent."

No doubt Nancy had a lot to offer. Her attributes were compelling, to say the least. But her unappealing expectations overrode her attractive virtues.

By being entitled, Nancy set herself up for failure. She was on the road to bitterness.

Despite their pretentiousness, entitled people live in utter fear of not having what they want.

Driven by this fear, entitled people ensure themselves the ultimate self-fulfilling prophecy. Either they don't get what they want, or it doesn't feel like enough. So they keep moving the finish line and wanting more. They keep not getting it and eventually become embittered.

What ensures an entitled person's self-fulfilling prophecy? Believing and/or acting as if they are entitled.

"Huh?" you say. "How does that make sense?"

Look to yourself for the answer. What's your response when encountering the demands of an entitled person? Do you want to give them what they want?

Usually not. In fact, quite the opposite. We usually don't want to give in to an entitled person's demands because we feel unconsidered and manipulated. We resent them. Worst case, we become bitter about them.

When an entitled person doesn't get what they want, they resent the people around them. When people feel resented, they resent back. Resentment breeds more resentment. Now the entitled person can make an even better case for bitterness.

Ultimately, the entitled person achieves their self-fulfilling prophecy: "No one will give them what they want." Their fear fills them with an even greater desperation, which ironically drives them to acting more entitled.

As stated in an earlier chapter, an entitled person is anyone whose demands exceed their willingness to do what's necessary. In this case, Nancy wanted life to give her what she wanted on her terms. Life wasn't playing along.

No matter what underlies a person's dissatisfaction, they will eventually snap.

Their anger will eventually prevail.

Their wants will eventually disappear.

And only their bitterness will remain.

Can you see how your dissatisfaction is leading you to bitterness?

_____

What reality do you keep refusing to acknowledge?

_____

What would you do differently if a genie, an angel, or a burning bush told you that you weren't going to get what you want?

_____

Choose appreciation over expectation.

Unwilling?

> "There was a time in Nancy's life that she wouldn't have noticed Peter."

That's what Nancy's sister said while toasting Nancy and Peter's engagement.

After dropping the notion that she was entitled to perfection, opening her eyes, and dating some of the most unlikely people, Nancy found herself happily engaged to Peter, the perfect man for her.

Prior to that time, Nancy was unwilling to consider other possibilities: other types of men to whom she could be attracted.

Our greatest gifts come from the most unexpected places. Sadly, we're usually afraid to look there.

We act as if our unwillingness is a choice. But it's not. It's fear. If it wasn't fear, then why not explore? Why not be willing to look and see?

As is true with all of our aberrations, unless we intervene in the underlying misperceptions, we repeat our mistakes. In the case of unwillingness, we misperceive ourselves as credible and claim to know better.

But in any area in which we're unhappy, how is it possible to think that we know better? Shouldn't the right to that claim belong to people who have actually been successful in those areas?

The more entrenched we become in our unwillingness, the more certain our failure. Have you ever met someone who refused to discuss their problems or seek advice? Did they suddenly find happiness? No. They never do.

The answer, as always, comes from exploring possibilities.

You can't explore if you're unwilling.

And you can't discover if you won't explore.

What possibilities have you been unwilling to explore?

_____

What would change for the better if you accepted that life is different from what you thought it should be?

_____

What should you be doing differently?

_____

Work on your peripheral vision and be willing to look in new directions.

Unrealistic?

Laura and Ken knew exactly what they wanted for their new kitchen and dining area.

A formal table would seat a dozen or more people.

A large kitchen island would offer enough surface space to accommodate keys, packages, groceries, and anything they wanted to remember to take on their way out.

All of the neighborhood kids could sit around the island and do art projects.

Laura could stand at the island and look out into the family room while cooking.

And whoever was stuck doing the dishes could also look out instead of staring at a wall.

It was the perfect design except for the fact that it was impossible to achieve.

There wasn't enough space for a massive dining room table and an island.

If there was a cooktop on the island, there would be no spot for a sink, let alone surface space for various belongings.

And also, if there was a cooktop on the island, it wouldn't always be safe for the kids to sit around and do art projects.

Laura and Ken were unrealistic about the space they had and about how much their kitchen island could accommodate. Once they confronted that reality, they were tremendously disappointed.

But their kitchen disappointment was just one of many.

Laura was disappointed about Ken getting out of shape even though she had contributed to his weight gain. When they first met, Ken regularly played basketball. He only stopped because Laura regularly complained about him not going to the mall with her instead.

Ken resented Laura for placing her work commitments over family obligations even though he was the one who chose to marry a professional woman with a high-paying career.

Laura's and Ken's unrealistic expectations are not at all uncommon. Sadly, it is quite normal for people to resent the realistic by-products of their partner's attributes and often of their own.

For instance...

If you were drawn to someone's boyish or girlish charms, they will likely have some immature behavior that goes with them.

If you were attracted to a self-made millionaire, you shouldn't be surprised when they're consumed by work.

If you chose someone because of their flawless beauty, you shouldn't be surprised to find them self-obsessed about their appearance.

If you successfully wooed someone with your money, you shouldn't be surprised by them wanting to spend it.

If you chose a competitive athlete or an Olympic hopeful, you shouldn't resent their workouts.

If you wanted someone passive, you shouldn't blame them for not making decisions.

If you partnered with an alpha, you shouldn't resent their propensity for always taking the lead.

If you picked someone religious, you shouldn't be surprised that they might be inclined to answer to a higher authority.

If you elected to be with a carefree artist, you shouldn't be surprised by their lack of money or career motivation, even when you start having kids.

If you married someone who was certain they didn't want kids, you shouldn't be surprised when they still don't want kids.

If you hooked up with someone who was too young to know better, you shouldn't be surprised when they grow old enough to figure it out.

If you were attracted to an adventurer, you shouldn't be surprised by their absence. They'll be off having adventures.

Likewise, if *you* are the adventurer, you can't always expect safety and absence of risk.

If you don't take care of your body, you can't be surprised when it doesn't stay healthy.

If you don't save for retirement, you will likely have less money than you'll need when the time comes.

These and the hundreds not listed are all blatantly obvious and perpetrated every moment of every day.

An unrealistic person's favorite lament is "If only..." It's a wish to change universal truths. And it never works because universal truths never change.

If only you were perfect.

If only you weren't born with the challenges you have.

If only your parents had done a better job.

If only you had figured life out earlier.

If only you had ——'s life.

If only you had made better decisions.

If only you could do it all over again.

If only...

What could be more unrealistic than wishing to change the past or the very fundamentals of someone's nature, including your own?

If you're unrealistic, your unhappiness is guaranteed.

Where are you being unrealistic in your life?

_____

What realities do you refuse to accept?

_____

Welcome reality.

Are You
Immature?

Helen arrived forty minutes late. It wasn't the first time. I didn't bother asking why, but she felt compelled to offer an excuse.

"I got lost," Helen explained.

"Uh-huh." I nodded.

"I thought Fifth Street would go through," she continued, "but..."

"It's a dead end," I finished for her.

"Well, I know that now," she snidely confirmed with a bit of attitude.

"But...?" I said with pause, knowing there was more to come.

"It makes no sense," she pontificated. "I don't see why all of the streets don't go through."

"Didn't something similar happen a few weeks ago?"

"Why, yes, that's yet another example," she cited.

"Did you ever look at a map?"

"No," she answered, looking perplexed. "Why would I do that?"

How many failed people have you heard giving their opinions about how they think things should be? Are they the ones people, other than fellow losers, want to listen to?

Driving and navigating your life are the same. It doesn't matter that you think it should be one way when in reality it's another. Our view of how we think something is does not supersede reality.

This is the difference between immaturity and maturity.

An immature person thinks they know how things should be.

A mature person knows how they are.

That doesn't mean a mature person needs to settle.

It only means that improvements are built upon realities.

Where do you listen to your own immaturity instead of reality?

_____

When do you give your opinions despite having no success?

_____

Choose observing over opining.

Mislabeled?

Jimmy introduced himself by telling me how inspirational he was. It wasn't just his view, I was told. According to Jimmy, everyone thought he was inspirational and frequently told him so.

I could not imagine anyone believing that Jimmy was inspirational, yet I'm sure no one was comfortable telling him otherwise.

I had to wait to correct Jimmy's self-labeling. No matter how ridiculous someone's misconception might be, it's unkind and ineffective to rip it away without giving them someplace else to stand.

Over the next several weeks, Jimmy continued to mention his great inspirational powers whenever he spoke. He told me that even the employees at his local gas station were inspired by him, as were all of his clients and all of the people with whom he worked.

After a short while, the perfect opportunity presented itself. Jimmy told a story about a success he had at work. He wrapped up the tale by attributing his success to how inspirational he was.

> "Actually," I jumped in, "your success has nothing to do with you being inspirational."

> "Huh?" Jimmy responded, visibly startled.

"What your story illustrates is that you're extremely diligent. In fact, every success that you have ever shared with me is based on your exceptional diligence."

Jimmy instantly felt the fit. His eyes lit up, and he never mentioned being inspirational again.

If Jimmy wanted to effect a change or increase his chances for success, thinking that he could crank up his nonexistent inspirational powers would lead him nowhere. On the other hand, cranking up his diligence would be tremendously effective.

People love labeling themselves. Calm. Shy. Patient. Funny. Powerful. Thoughtful. Intelligent. Spiritual.

When the pressure goes up, the inaccurate labeling is revealed, and the alleged attributes are nowhere to be found. The allegedly calm go crazy. The allegedly patient fly off the handle. And so forth.

No matter which labels you might choose, you can't utilize attributes that you don't have.

We cannot be effective believing, labeling, or advertising ourselves to have attributes that we do not possess.

That doesn't mean we can't grow and evolve. We just can't declare anything before it's true.

Besides, once we have a virtue, we don't need to label and declare it. People will notice it on their own.

How do you mislabel yourself?

_____

What attributes do you claim to have?

_____

What attributes would other people say you have?

_____

Listen to what the world is saying.
Invite people to say more.
Work with what you hear.

Compensating?

"Everyone said I was POWERFUL," Brandy boasted after a group exercise of people sharing their reactions to one another.

"Nope," I intervened, "not a single person said you were powerful. They said you were overpowering."

"THAT'S... NOT... TRUE!!!" Brandy disclaimed, enunciating each word.

Brandy was no stranger to exclamation points and loved speaking in uppercase.

"YES... IT... IS!!!" I answered in matching cadence.

"I'M BOLD!" Brandy countered, leaning forward in her chair.

"No, Brandy. You're brash."

"I'M A FREE SPIRIT!" Brandy persisted.

"No, Brandy. You take people hostage by your need to be seen. There's nothing freeing about you."

People mistakenly believe that they can declare who they are regardless of whether it's true. In their misguided attempts, they are declaring who they are not.

Either we have a virtue or we don't. Some virtues we might be able to develop. Some we cannot. To develop something, we first have to admit that we don't have it.

Developing an absent virtue is hard work, so some go for what they believe is the next best thing. That's what Brandy did.

Brandy didn't feel heard, so she compensated — actually overcompensated — with brashness. She didn't feel powerful, so she went with what she thought was the next best thing: overpowering.

Brandy deluded herself into thinking that her vices were the next best thing to the virtues she coveted. They're not. Vices are the antitheses of virtues.

Admitting that we don't have a virtue is usually not a problem. It's simply an asset we don't have. Conversely, overcompensating for an asset's absence, as Brandy did, creates a liability.

Typically, the most blatant compensations, such as Brandy's, are either tolerated by people who are uncomfortable pointing them out or are encouraged by those with equally obvious compensations. The conspiracy to support one another in the charade is the basis of many cliques.

There are some less obvious compensations that we regularly miss. For instance, we all know people who are always there in a pinch. We can call them night or day, and they will bend over backward to help out. Many of these people are simply fantastic human beings. However, there are others who relish being seen as saints, while their closest friends and family suffer their neglect.

In other words, virtuous isn't always so virtuous. It could be a vice in disguise.

Whenever you need to be seen in a particular way, whether you're successful at pulling it off or not, you are compensating for a feared deficiency that you don't want to address.

Where are you compensating for virtues you wish you had?

_____

Which vices have you mislabeled as virtues?

_____

Which virtues are concealing vices?

_____

What are you trying to hide?

_____

Stop pretending.

Overrated?

"I don't know why I didn't get a callback," Tony said about his television audition. "I was fantastic!"

"How do you know?" I asked.

"I could feel it," Tony assured.

"Have you ever been hired from a television audition?"

"Well, no, but that's just because they don't get me," Tony explained. "They just won't give me a chance."

"Why do you think that is?"

"They don't want to take any risks. They just want to play it safe. That's why they won't hire me to star in a movie."

"Really?" I challenged. "You think you have the chops to carry a motion picture?"

"Yep," Tony bragged with cocky confidence, "I have a real commanding presence."

"That's interesting. If you have such a commanding presence, how come you can't get an agent?"

Most failed actors have an abundance of reasons for not getting work. Most failed comics think their lack of success is the audience's fault. It's the same with anyone who claims the world doesn't appreciate their brilliance.

Just because we declare something doesn't mean it's true. Just because someone doesn't disagree with us also doesn't mean it's true. It's important to consider the source.

Many wannabe performers find themselves to be much more entertaining than the rest of us do. Just because, when they were seven, their mother and aunt sat on the couch enjoying their one-person show doesn't mean they were talented. It probably means their mother and aunt were both very sweet.

It was obvious to everyone that Tony was only fantastic in his own mind. But in his world, the director and casting director just didn't get it. It was their deficiency, not his.

The world is telling you what it thinks. You can't outshout it.

As stated earlier, just because you declare it doesn't make it so.

Just because you put time into it doesn't make it so.

Just because you want it really, really badly also doesn't make it so.

There are apparent exceptions. We have all seen superstar performers who claim that everyone told them to give up and that it was only their perseverance that kept them going. They love telling their fans to be who they are and to never give up.

There are a couple of problems with their claims and proclamations. First of all, it's unlikely that every single credible person told them to give up. And second, many of these superstars are phenomenally talented.

Millions of people wish they were athletes, performers, and millionaires. Hundreds of thousands make the attempt. But nothing gets around the fact that there has to be reality and a substantial dose of potential in your dream. Otherwise, it's just a fantasy.

My favorite quote about fantasies comes from my friend Breck...

> "Our fantasies must die for our dreams to come true."

The hands-down number one problem that I witness is people wishing to be who they are not. The problem with wishing to be who you are not is losing the benefits of who you really are.

Whenever I point out someone's grandiose overrating, their first response is disbelief. That quickly transitions to resentment. And then a moment later, they move to entitlement.

Nine times out of ten, when I point out aspects of someone's true self, they instantly want to change it. No exploration. They simply want it removed as if it were a wart.

Why do people so desperately want to change who they are? It conflicts with their childhood conclusions of how they need to be seen.

Some people underrate themselves.

Some overrate.

Underrating ends in despair.

Overrating ends in anger.

How do you overrate yourself?

_____

How do you underrate yourself?

_____

What should you be verifying with others?

_____

What are the motives of the people who are telling you what you want to hear?

_____

Distinguish between people who really do agree with you and those who are jockeying to have you agree with them.

Implausible?

"Don't eat that!" Elise screamed.

"Pardon me?" Barry replied with surprise. He had never met this woman, yet she had no compunction about dictating the content of his buffet plate.

"That's high in saturated fat, so you want to stay away from that," Elise continued lecturing. "And you definitely don't want to eat that roll. I'm certain it's not gluten-free."

"Actually," Barry replied, "I'm really okay with my selections here."

"Well, suit yourself," Elise fired back in a huff before storming off.

"That's so weird," Barry muttered to himself, as he continued assembling his plate.

Barry was right. It was weird. Actually, it was preposterous.

Barry, a former NFL quarterback, was as lean as they come and in perfect physical condition. There was nothing he couldn't eat in moderation or, for that matter, even without moderation.

As Barry left the buffet table, he spotted Elise standing near the piano and lecturing another unwitting party guest. It was difficult to know which would tip the scale more: Elise or the piano.

This is not a comment about Elise's weight. It's a comment about her credibility. Despite having her obvious implausibility, despite having spent most of her life trying to lose weight over the course of two dozen different diets, Elise refused to recognize that she had no credibility even when talking to someone who was clearly in superior shape.

Elise is not unique. She's no different from the actors working in restaurants who think they know best about film.

Or the couch potatoes who know how world-class athletes should play their sports.

Or the men who know best about women's reproductive rights.

Or the perpetually unemployed who know how corporations should be run.

Or the critics, failed in their own craft, who know better than the artists they're critiquing.

Independent of whether someone is believable or not, there's one thing all self-proclaimed experts seem to ignore...

Credibility cannot be seized. It can only be granted.

How are you implausible?

_____

Is there anyone without ulterior motives or fear of hurting your feelings who buys it?

_____

In what areas have you produced enough results to prove your credibility?

_____

**Stop talking as if you have success
in the areas that you do not.**

Incredulous?

"I think you need to be more careful," I cautioned. "Perhaps you shouldn't be making these decisions."

"What do you mean?"

"Bob, you just lost $300,000 in another bad investment."

"So?"

"So doesn't that tell you something?"

"It happens," Bob excused.

"Yes, but it happens more to you. Can you see the possibility that you might not know what you're doing?"

"Screw you! I can't believe you'd say that to me."

Despite all evidence to the contrary, Bob had convinced himself that his monetary setback was an anomaly even though it was strikingly similar to all of the other identical anomalies.

Bob was able to ignore the most important question we can ever ask ourselves.

It's the question that reveals whether we have the self-attributed talents that we claim or those told to us by people with as little or less credibility as we or by people who have an ulterior motive or a misplaced sense of kindness.

It's the question whose answer speaks for itself.

It's the question that an incredulous person never wants to ask.

It's the question avoided like Kryptonite.

The question is...

"How's that working out for you?"

Incredulous people attempt to deny the truth at all costs, especially when it gets in the way of their point of view.

They value what is self-righteous over what should be self-evident. And they fight for philosophy over reality — how they think it *should* be versus how it really is.

The incredulous person's most frequent battle cry is "How dare you?"

They mask their embarrassment by choosing dissension over humility and graciousness.

And it's that very dissension that ultimately leads to their descent.

When do you get incredulous?

_____

What do you refuse hear?

_____

What are you embarrassed to hear?

_____

Who has tried to tell you?

_____

What would happen if you admitted the truth?

_____

Admit the truth.

Wounded?

Phil was shouting at the top of his lungs. His wife had just told him that attending his basketball game wasn't important, which of course meant that he wasn't important.

In reality, Janey said, "Honey, I'm not sure I can make it to the game in time." But from Phil's perspective, Janey had just told him he didn't matter.

Phil had grown up being invisible. He was raised by the household staff and saw his parents only on occasion. They didn't know what sports he played or what his college major was. They didn't attend a single graduation and had never met their youngest grandchild.

Phil was understandably wounded, as he would be the first to admit. And yet he continued to drive himself into a rage by what he thought Janey was saying. Time and time again, Phil would adamantly swear upon the accuracy of his perceptions and accusations.

The cycle was always the same. Phil would think he was hearing what was never being said, and Janey would quickly jump to her own defense. The battles consistently escalated to allegations that neither listened to the other, with both of them yelling full volume.

Phil needed to acknowledge that he wasn't credible when hearing any form of "no". He also needed to be more responsible in what he said next. For example, he could have told Janey, "I know that you said you might not be able to make it on time, but what I heard in my own head is that you don't care."

If Phil could manage to not start off with an accusation, Janey could take care of him instead of worrying about protecting herself. But that couldn't happen unless Phil was willing to acknowledge the effects of his wound even when the admission was inconvenient.

People tend to conveniently remember their wounds when it suits them. They respond with "You can't talk to me that way" when they don't want to listen to you and with "What wound?" when they expect you to listen to them.

It might be obvious what an emotional "wound" is, but let's be sure. In the context of this work, most people would say that someone is wounded by bad events from their childhood. For instance, if someone was beaten, then that would form an emotional wound.

In reality, that's not what causes an emotional wound. There are plenty of people who had worse situations than we had but didn't seem to suffer the same long-term damage. Conversely, there are many who had a much easier childhood yet are severely traumatized.

Consistent with what we have been discussing, an emotional wound is when an observation becomes a dire conclusion. For instance, if you are criticized as a child, that doesn't form the wound. But the moment you conclude that you will continue to be criticized for whatever you do or that you always deserve the criticism, then you have an emotional wound.

I say this because, just like their physical counterparts, emotional wounds get protected. Almost every behavior that has been discussed relates to people wanting to protect themselves from the pain they suffered during childhood. They're tending to their emotional wounds.

In other words, they are trying to protect themselves from the conclusions that they reached. "I'm going to get punished" or "I'm going to get punished if I ——."

If they had never been concerned about recurrence, they would have never developed behavior to protect against it. So from that perspective, there's no emotional wound.

That's not to say there's no memory of what happened or no lessons learned. It's just that the person isn't driven by the same hypervigilance and need to guard themselves as someone who is emotionally wounded.

Emotional wounds are at the top of the list of things most people would like to rid themselves of. Of course, it's not possible. The past isn't changing.

And while it would be insane to wish those emotional wounds upon anyone, once they are there, they become an opportunity for growth and connection.

We are all connected by pain. Our closest friends are the ones with whom we can share it. We can attract admirers by being entertaining, impressive, through flattery, etc. But heart-to-heart connections only come from sharing the depth of pain.

Ironically, Janey fell in love with Phil because of his emotional wound. It was their very first date.

> "How was your day?" Phil asked to get the
> conversation started.

"I don't mean to be a downer," Janey sighed, "but it wasn't good. I almost canceled, but I was really looking forward to our date."

"Tell me," Phil begged with tears forming in his eyes. "What happened?"

At that moment, Janey thought to herself...

"Wow. He knows pain. This is a man I can trust."

Phil's painful wound connected him to his heart. His heart connected him to Janey's. Isn't it ironic that he would want to hide the number one reason that Janey fell in love with him?

Phil was embarrassed of his emotional wound. Janey valued it. Our past can't change, but our response to it can. With assistance, Phil could have learned to embrace his wound.

Life is all about being vulnerable and bold. Vulnerability without boldness is weak. Boldness without vulnerability is brash.

With heart and intelligence, your emotional wounds can become your greatest assets. They have the power to give you depth, compassion, empathy, and humility.

Your acceptance, your commitment, *and* your pain form the perfect balance of vulnerability and boldness.

Don't be ashamed of your emotional wounds.

Don't flaunt them.

Accept them.

Contribute with them.

What emotional wounds are you not acknowledging?

_____

How have they made you a better person?

_____

How can you contribute with them?

_____

What has changed since the wounds were originally formed?

_____

Use your wounds to open your heart.

Deceptive?

They were having the same argument they always had. Jim scheduled another business trip for the weekend, leaving Maria to attend another family event on her own. Even worse, it was Jim's family that was having the get-together.

> "Jeez, if I would have known it was so important to you, I would have postponed the trip. You should have told me, Maria."

> "I should have told you? Are you kidding? It's *your* family! And I told you a half-dozen times!" Maria exclaimed in utter frustration.

> "Sorry, hon, I just didn't know."

> Maria threw up her hands.

> "What the hell is that for?" Jim barked. "I told you I was sorry."

For the first few years of their marriage, Maria fell for Jim's deception.

Jim would act without consideration and feign ignorance, and Maria would repeat all of the reasons for wanting what she wanted.

Then Jim would feign listening, promise it wouldn't happen again, and repeat his behavior a few weeks later.

Finally, Maria caught on.

Jim exercised the perfect deception: playing dumb.

When we are repeating a loop in any area of our lives, it's likely we're acting as if we don't know something. We probably just don't want to admit it.

To get around admitting it, we use our alleged ignorance to lure others into the wrong conversation, just like Jim did with Maria.

Jim didn't want to admit that he knew what he was doing when he scheduled a trip and left Maria to attend another family get-together on her own. It would lead to a conversation about his selfishness.

So instead, Jim pretended not to know in hopes of having a different conversation. He was much more willing to argue about not listening than discuss his selfishness. That way, he could continue doing what he wanted.

Jim is not unique. Have you ever noticed how well it works out for you when you deceive people into believing that you don't know what you really do know?

Somehow, you always get to do what you want.

How do you use deception to get what you want?

_____

What are the things you claim to not know?

_____

What should you be doing that you're not doing?

_____

Tell the truth.

Trapped?

Sandra was living with Rod, and Rod was beating Sandra. All of the signs were there.

She applied too much makeup around her eyes.

He had bruises on his knuckles.

She wore long-sleeved dresses on the hottest of days.

He looked at her with disdain.

And Sandra had a nervous twitch whenever Rod moved or even spoke.

Sandra believed she had two options: She could stay with Rod, and he would eventually realize his love for her and stop beating her. Or she could leave Rod and be alone for the rest of her life.

In reality, those weren't Sandra's actual choices. Neither scenario was possible. By attempting to choose between two invalid choices, Sandra kept herself trapped.

Sandra's real choices were to stay with Rod and likely end up dead. Or she could leave Rod and have at least a 50 percent chance of meeting someone else.

Whether you go with the tactic of claiming not to know what you really do know or choosing between two invalid options, the result is the same. You will be forever trapped.

Why is it a "tactic"? Because while Sandra might say that she hopes for something to be different, her childhood conclusions, such as "I don't deserve to be treated kindly," are in control.

Sandra doesn't see any other possibility. She will act as if she understands what you're saying, but you might as well be speaking Martian.

In Sandra's mind, she is getting what she deserves. She's trapped in her childhood conclusions.

As has been said many times about many people, Sandra is not unique. Granted, her situation might be more severe than that of many others, but most everyone is trapped to a degree.

Perhaps the word "trapped" is leading you astray. Maybe you know it by its aliases: "patterns", "habits", "style", and "destiny".

You don't need to ask what's inside the trap because you probably already know the answer. It's you.

So instead, let's think about what's outside the trap.

It's the life you could be living.

Where do you feel trapped?

_____

What possibilities are you ignoring?

_____

What don't you allow yourself to think?

_____

Whom should you be listening to for advice?

_____

Whom should you not be listening to?

_____

**Don't let others treat you badly.
Get assistance when you need help.**

Evasive?

Walter was five foot seven and 340 pounds.

One evening, he showed up at Robin and Debby's house crying. His doctor had just told Walter that if his diabetes didn't kill him, his overtaxed heart would.

Through his sobs, Walter shared his disbelief.

> "How could this be happening to me?" Walter wailed.

Robin and Debby weren't surprised. How could Walter be?

For the better part of his life, Walter had successfully utilized the tactics discussed in the previous chapters. He claimed to somehow not know that his weight (which he obviously did not gain overnight) and diabetes (for which he had been under treatment for fifteen years) were problems.

There were occasions in which Walter discussed changing his diet. But in his mind, his only choice was between eating what he wanted (thus being able to enjoy life) or going on a diet (thus forgoing all pleasure).

But now with his doctor's prognosis, Walter would finally have the motivation to take the appropriate actions and choose a healthier path. Unfortunately, that's not what happened. Instead...

Walter pleaded for advice to get himself in better shape.

Robin answered Walter's plea by sharing her simple technique of starting with walks and eliminating sugar from her diet.

Walter rejected it.

> "No way. That's too easy. I need to do more than that."

Since Walter dismissed Robin's program as too easy, Debby tried to tell Walter about her exercise classes. But before she could finish her second sentence, Walter rejected the notion.

> "No way. That's too hard. I couldn't possibly do that much."

And with those two responses, Walter successfully derailed his chances. Walter ensured being stuck.

By declaring one solution as too easy and the other as too hard, Walter left himself with nothing to do. The plan worked perfectly.

Here's how it's done:

> Claim you don't know.

> Choose between two wrong answers.

> Or declare any solution as too easy or too hard.

The previous two chapters illustrated the first two tactics. Walter went with the third.

Any one of these simple techniques will keep you stuck forever.

Can you see how these behaviors would leave Walter stuck?

Can you imagine how these behaviors might fit perfectly with Walter's childhood observations and conclusions?

Walter's dad died of diabetes-related complications when Walter was eleven. Can you fill in the rest?

Walter's conclusion was that he was going to die young. In accepting this conclusion, his solution was to let himself do whatever he wanted. After all, it wouldn't matter anyhow.

Walter had set up the perfect self-fulfilling prophecy.

If there is something that you have said you want to change...

And if it actually is possible to change...

And if you are not changing it...

It's because you are declaring the necessary action to be too easy or too hard...

And you are believing a faulty observation, conclusion, and/or solution from your childhood.

By evading reality, you keep yourself stuck (or worse).

Which solutions are you evading with the excuse that they're too easy?

_____

Which solutions are you evading with the excuse that they're too hard?

_____

**Be honest about what you are willing to do
and accept the consequences of your decisions.**

Manipulative?

After listening to her friend Walter evade taking any action to solve his health problems, Robin noticed...

"Walter, you're ignoring all of our suggestions."

"It's... it's... just that... that... I'm so ashamed," Walter announced before bursting into tears.

"Oh my god!" Robin wailed. "I'm so sorry."

Ding. Ding. Ding. Ding. Walter scored the biggie. He pulled out the Shame Card.

If something is shameful, it's sacred. And if it's sacred, it proclaims to all around...

"Don't you DARE speak of this."

And the threat works. Most people back off immediately.

Telling people that you are ashamed is a fantastic defensive act, no different from a child crying before getting punished.

They're trying to make you believe that they're already suffering. You're supposed to feel guilty and let them off the hook.

That's what Shame Throwers do. They make you feel guilty about their pain. And then what you're supposed to do, if you are a decent human being, is let them get away with whatever they want.

Here's the test: In those moments, if someone is able to tell you about their shame without breaking into a sweat, physically shaking, coming close to hyperventilating, and without their throat constricted to the point that they sound as if they're choking, then it's not shame.

It might be embarrassment. But just as likely, it's inconvenience masquerading as embarrassment or shame in order to get what it wants.

How can that be known? Because every single time someone pulls out the Shame Card — I cannot emphasize it enough: every SINGLE time — the person somehow, coincidentally, luck of the draw, just so happens, never fails to get exactly what they want.

Walter didn't want to exercise, so he said what he needed to say to get out of it. If he was really ashamed, he would take action to address it. He would not do something to perpetrate it.

Does this sound heartless? Personally, I think it would be heartless to condone Walter killing himself with his own BS.

If you think otherwise and if you're playing the Shame Card this very moment, then ask yourself how that has been working out for you.

Have you noticed how long your shame has persisted? If so, then ask yourself whether you would like to continue being right or whether you'd actually like to move forward.

If you prefer, you could continue to do what you always do. You could try to convince people of your point. You can make a case that your shame is sacred and shouldn't be questioned.

Okay, you're right. Now what?

The answer is your pain persists. Congratulations.

Let's try something else. You're wrong. Now what?

The answer is a possibility for a better life.

By the way, it's completely okay to leave areas of your life unaddressed. Just don't profess that you want to or are addressing them when you really are not. Save yourself, and those around you, a chunk of time and admit that you're going to let it ride.

If you are willing to live with the consequences of your decisions, then stop the pretense that you are addressing those things that you really are not. This will give you, and everyone around you, some relief.

We use shame to restrict ourselves and manipulate others. Is the trade-off worth it?

True shame is a tremendously horrible burden.

It's not one you should bear on your own.

Nor should it be used as an offensive weapon against yourself...

...or a defensive weapon against others.

How do you manipulate people with your shame in order to get what you want?

_____

What would others tell you if they weren't afraid of crossing that line you drew?

_____

If you're feeling shame, whose assistance should you seek to address it?

_____

Make the choice between flaunting your shame and healing it.

Unable?

It had been a week since Chuck admitted that he had given money to an unworthy recipient. It wasn't his first time, and his friend Howard was afraid it wouldn't be his last.

"Chuck, let me get this straight," Howard began. "After everything that has happened, do you still think that you're able to decide whom you should be giving money to?"

"First of all, they're 'loans', not 'giveaways'," Chuck arrogantly declared. "And second, yes, of course I do."

"I think you're operating with the wrong definition of a loan," Howard retorted. "Loans get paid back."

"I misspoke," Chuck quickly amended. "They're investments."

"Your 'investments'" — Howard punctuated with air quotes — "have lost you a million dollars. So what makes you think that you're good with money?"

"Well, because I'm really careful about spending," Chuck explained.

"On what? Amazon?"

Chuck was stunned at being caught. "Umm, yeah."

"Let me ask you this, Chuck. Why are you doing this?"

Chuck thought about it long and hard before answering, "To change people's lives for the better. What good am I if I can't do that?"

Chuck, like most everyone else you have been told about, was trying to solve a childhood problem. He grew up believing he didn't make a difference. So he decided that he would improve people's lives. But by giving money to the wrong people, Chuck wasn't making the contribution he intended.

Wanting to help people is a worthwhile aspiration, but Chuck picked an area in which he had no discernment. He had the resources, but given his lack of judgment, he wouldn't have those assets for long.

If Howard would have explored further, Chuck might have admitted that what he really wanted was to be loved.

Of course, we all want to be loved. Unfortunately, whether Chuck had the necessary financial acumen or not, his solution wasn't going to provide what he was looking for. Giving away money wouldn't lead to him being loved. At the very best, it might lead to him being appreciated.

Being loved comes from someone seeing who you are, not what you do.

In what areas do you operate as if you are able when you really are not able?

_____

Do you think it's possible to feel loved without your real and alleged abilities?

_____

Contribute in a manner that enhances who you are.

Pretending?

Jackson had just started a new job. He was managing a group of PhD scientists who were building a component for the International Space Station.

Although Jackson was an excellent manager, with ample experience to contribute, he didn't have a PhD and wondered whether that would be a problem for his new staff.

"I'm glad to meet you," Jackson said to Michelle, one of the supervisors who worked for him.

"Me too. Welcome aboard. I guess you'd like to talk about what I do."

"That would be great," Jackson responded.

Literally within thirty seconds of starting, Jackson realized that he didn't know what Michelle was talking about it. She realized it too.

"Um, my apologies," Michelle offered. "Are you familiar with this technology?"

"No, I'm not," Jackson readily admitted. "I don't know a thing about it."

"Would you like me to explain it to you?"

"Please. That would be wonderful."

Michelle began explaining the fundamentals.

> "Is this making sense?" Michelle inquired. "Am I being too simplistic?"

> "Gosh, no," Jackson assured. "You couldn't make it too simple. Please pretend you're talking to an idiot."

You might think that this was the worst thing that could have happened. Here Jackson was, meeting his first subordinate, and his ignorance about the details of her work was plain as day. It certainly wasn't the encounter he was hoping for. However...

Because Jackson didn't pretend to know something that he didn't, Michelle discovered that her new boss was someone who easily admitted what he didn't know.

Jackson's self-effacing manner and openness also told Michelle that he was interested in learning from her.

Jackson's confidence, even in the face of not knowing something, led Michelle to the conclusion that he had things he could teach her.

Jackson's graciousness made Michelle comfortable.

Jackson's lack of pretense set the foundation for a trusting relationship.

Jackson didn't have to pretend to be an expert in order to garner respect. It was the opposite. Jackson's acknowledgment of what he didn't know earned Michelle's respect.

Lastly, Jackson's interest in learning from Michelle increased her interest in learning what Jackson knew. In fact, as the meeting progressed, Michelle realized that Jackson's macro-knowledge far exceeded hers. She was focused on a single aspect of the research, as were her colleagues. Meanwhile, Jackson, although brand-new, seemed to have a vision for how everyone's work could be tied together. In the past, each person's efforts never progressed beyond individual research. It became apparent to Michelle that Jackson knew exactly how to meld the individual efforts into a cohesive result.

At the conclusion of their meeting, Jackson checked with Michelle...

> "Are there any questions I can answer for you?"

> "Just one," Michelle replied. "It's refreshing to talk to someone who's so open about what he doesn't know. Aren't you worried that someone could use that against you, especially when you're starting a new job?"

> "Nah. You were so kind in the way you asked me if I understood what you were talking about that I had no hesitation. Besides, when Charles originally offered me the job, I remember thanking him and saying, 'You apparently think you have a lot of reasons for hiring me. And I appreciate that. But before you make that offer, I want to make sure you know all of the reasons why that might not be such a good idea.'"

> "You're kidding," Michelle laughed. "What did he say?"

> "He laughed just like you did."

Jackson was hired because his boss saw the importance of virtues that Jackson had not fully valued in himself. His disarming honesty for one, not to mention the other abilities that Michelle quickly discovered.

If you are occupied pretending to have virtues that you do not, there's a good chance you're not noticing or valuing the virtues you do have.

What do you pretend in order to be liked or respected?

_____

What would happen if you admitted the truth?

_____

Harness the virtues you already have.

145

Lost?

Martin's wife had just left him. It had been a long time coming. He wouldn't take advice or direction from anyone. Not his friends. Not his wife. Not me. Not anyone.

Despite all evidence to the contrary, Martin still believed that he knew best.

> "Are you upset?" I asked.

> "What do you think?" he snarled.

> "Are you willing to hear some advice?"

> "No, I already know what I'm going to do," Martin declared, immediately followed by a ten-minute tirade.

When Martin finally stopped talking, I asked again...

> "Are you upset?"

> "Yes, damn it. I'm upset. Why the hell do you keep asking me that?"

> "Well, your life is collapsing around you. It played out as everyone warned. You continued doing what you wanted. And yet you haven't asked anyone a single question about what you should do. Instead,

despite your miserable track record, you just spent ten minutes telling me your solution."

"Okay," he conceded.

"So I just have one question for you."

"Am I upset?" Martin sarcastically imitated.

"No, that's not what I was going to ask. I'm just wondering why you keep going to yourself for advice when you clearly don't know what the hell you're talking about."

The thing we rarely consider is that the voices in our head, the ones coming up with solutions for our problems, are often the same voices that created the problems in the first place.

Where are you lost and not admitting it?

_____

Do you go to people for advice?

_____

Are they the right people?

_____

Only take direction from your successful self and others who are successful.

Stubborn?

Jerry arrived a defeated man.

"What happened?" I inquired.

"I lost the suit," he bemoaned.

"You mean the one against the contractor who remodeled your bathroom?"

"No. That was the one before," Jerry corrected.

"Oh yeah, that's right. This was the business client who violated the contract," I pretended to realize.

"No, that was the time before," Jerry clarified.

"Wait, how many lawsuits have you filed?"

"Eight," Jerry admitted.

"How many have you lost?"

"Eight."

"How many of those were you told to drop?"

"Eight," Jerry whispered.

"Gosh," I lamented, "if only you had someone you came to for advice."

"That's why I come to you," Jerry earnestly replied without recognizing the irony.

It does no good to seek advice that you're going to ignore. You waste everyone's time.

Stubborn equals stuck.

What advice have you been stubbornly ignoring?

_____

Whose time have you been wasting?

_____

**Step off your position
in order to see a different view.**

Idiotic?

"Mark's such an idiot," Lisa declared. "I can't believe I put up with his shit."

"All right. What do you want to do about it?"

"I'll tell you what I WON'T do," Lisa emphasized. "I won't be doing a damn thing until he apologizes."

"What are the chances of that?" I asked.

"Like slim to none. He doesn't even know what an idiot he is. And if he did, it wouldn't matter because he wouldn't apologize anyhow."

"I understand. So you're an idiot."

"What? What do you mean I'm an idiot? He's the idiot. He's off playing baseball. He doesn't even know that anything is wrong."

"No, really, I understand, Lisa. You're being an idiot."

"How can you say that?"

"Well, let's review. You declared that Mark is an idiot, right?"

"Yes."

"And you're saying that he's such an idiot and so unaware that he doesn't even know that what he has done is out of line."

"Uh-huh."

"Plus you're telling me that if he did know, he probably wouldn't do anything about it anyhow because he doesn't care or he's irresponsible or whatever. So while you're here suffering, he's off having a good time. And that's why you're waiting for Mark to make the first move."

"Exactly."

"Okay then. So what you're telling me is that you're placing your prospects for attaining resolution into the hands of a person you think is an unaware, uncaring, selfish idiot."

Lisa's mouth dropped open.

"How smart does that sound to you?" I advanced. "Doesn't it make more sense to entrust your well-being to someone for whom you have a higher regard?"

"Well, what I am supposed to do?"

"The first thing you need to do is acknowledge what you have always known. If you believe Mark is an idiot, then ask yourself whether you want to be in a relationship with an idiot."

"He's great at some things, but he sucks at others."

"That's also fine and human, by the way. And since you know the areas in which he sucks, that means you don't get to be upset."

"What?"

"In sports, an 'upset' is when the underdog wins. It's not a surprise or an 'upset' if the underdog loses just like everyone thought they would."

"So you're telling me that I can't be upset by Mark's stupid behavior because it's not a surprise?"

"Yes. It's the old adage 'Fool me once, shame on you. Fool me twice, shame on me.'"

"But I don't want to put up with that," Lisa declared.

"You don't have to. You can leave whenever you want. Or you and Mark can see whether both of you can resolve your problems. But what you shouldn't do is pretend that you're upset about something you already know. Your frustration isn't with Mark. You're frustrated with yourself for allowing yourself to be treated in a way that you don't like."

"That's true."

"Then it's back in your court. Mark might not be able to fix what you need him to fix. So you have to decide whether you are willing to live with that."

"Should I?"

"That's your call. If it continues to cause you pain, then no. If it's not getting better, then no. If you are constantly upset and suffering, then also no. And if you are diminishing yourself, then absolutely no. But if you can accept Mark's deficiency, then that's your call."

"You have no opinion?" Lisa begged to know.

"My opinion is that you should separate Mark's behavior from his heart."

"I'm having trouble imagining what that looks like."

"I'll give you an analogy. Many years ago, I received a fruit and cheese snack while on an airline flight, and I noticed that the woman next to me was having trouble chewing the Gouda. Do you know why?"

Lisa chuckled. "Because she didn't know she was supposed to remove the wax?"

"Exactly. Mark's behavior is the wax. His intent is the cheese. You have to decide whether the wax is too thick in contrast to the worthwhileness of the cheese. Separate Mark's aberrant psychology from what's in his heart. And no matter what, make sure that he's a person who can nurture you in a way that you deserve and in a manner that's healthy."

"Otherwise, *I'm* the idiot," Lisa laughed.

Where are you being idiotic by placing your happiness and well-being in the wrong person's hands?

_____

Who are the people who care about you?

_____

Who are the people who care more about themselves?

_____

**Only entrust your well-being
to people who deserve your trust.**

Demanding?

Merrill, who lifts weights at the gym several times a week, noticed that he was getting easily winded doing chores around his house. So he decided that he needed to change his exercise routine and focus on his endurance.

Merrill lessened the amount of weight that he lifted and increased his time on the treadmill. And a mere two weeks later, he noticed that he was less easily winded. Mission accomplished.

You would think that Merrill would be pleased. But he wasn't. He noticed that he had more endurance, but he lamented his slightly smaller biceps.

Merrill was using the wrong measure. He devoted himself to improving his endurance, yet he was measuring his effort by the size of his muscles. In so doing, he was demanding the impossible.

Similarly, consider parents who leave or reduce their time in the work world in order to raise their children. Should they criticize themselves for making less money? Of course not. The measure is the health of their kids. Salary, career, and status should not be the measure. But is that what many stay-at-home parents believe? Nope. They lament their lost career. It's the wrong measure and unfairly demanding.

On the other side of the same example, adults who don't leave the work world often measure themselves on a parenting scale. They regret not having kids or not having enough time with them.

If you use the right measure, you accept trade-offs.

If you don't, you checkmate yourself into perpetual demand.

When you deviate from a plan, you criticize yourself.

When you achieve results in one area, you criticize yourself for lacking results in another.

You can be demanding or happy.

It's one or the other.

How are you demanding?

_____

How does that adversely affect you?

_____

How does it adversely affect the people around you?

_____

Where could you replace your demands with inspiration?

_____

**Be comfortable with the by-product
of your choices.**

Procrastinating?

Mimi claimed she was going to write a book. As a successful therapist, she was certain that she had something to offer her readers.

During our meeting, Mimi frantically started detailing a litany of things she needed to do before she could begin writing.

> "I need to get an editor to help me organize, a graphic artist to help me illustrate it, a new computer to help me write, and someone to show me how to use the new software."

Mimi was overwhelmed and virtually incapacitated.

> "Let's begin with the basics," I suggested. "How about organizing your thoughts on three-by-five index cards?"

> "No no, that won't work," Mimi protested. "I need to get a new computer before I can even start thinking about the book."

> "Why?"

> "I don't know. I just do."

> "Didn't you write your PhD thesis on your current computer?"

"Yes," Mimi admitted.

"Are you saying that your book is going to be more complicated than your thesis?"

"No, of course not."

"Then why won't your old computer work for writing your book?"

"Well, I guess it would," Mimi seemed to realize.

"Fantastic. Now you can start."

Mimi calmed down. But the moment of calmness quickly disappeared as Mimi self-agitated herself.

"Oh my gosh, I have so much to write. I don't know where to begin."

"Didn't you just give a lecture on this topic?" I inquired.

"Yes."

"Wasn't it a raving success?"

"Yes."

"Wasn't it recorded on videotape?"

"Yes."

"So why don't you get the videotape and have someone transcribe it? You'd have the backbone for the entire book."

Mimi stared at me blankly.

"Mimi, it's straightforward," I explained. "We know your lecture was well organized because it was so popular. That gives you someplace to start."

"But what about the illustrator?" Mimi interrupted.

"You're not ready for that yet. Start with drawing stick figures until you're further along in the process."

"But what about my computer?"

The cycle continued for nearly an hour. Mimi's recycled concerns kept popping up like a game of Whac-a-Mole.

New concerns popped up just as quickly. At one point, Mimi was worried about the color of the book jacket.

Mimi left with a commitment to get the video of her previous lecture. She never did.

Our conversation took place nearly fifteen years ago. Not surprisingly, there is no book. However, there have been five new computers and countless software lessons.

Mimi didn't need a new computer nor software lessons. She didn't need to worry about an illustrator. Mimi just needed to start.

By "start", I don't mean on the book. Mimi needed to begin by addressing her resistance. Despite all of her claims, Mimi didn't really believe she could write a book. Fifteen years later, she continues to be right.

When most people make a to-do list, they tackle the items of lesser importance first. You might use the excuse that you're making room for the most important tasks. It's simply not true. You're avoiding them.

We think of procrastination as something we're *not* doing.

That's not the case.

Procrastination is the result of something we're not acknowledging.

In what areas of your life are you procrastinating?

_____

What do you keep doing instead of the thing you know you need to do?

_____

Can you accept that maybe you don't really want to do or think you can do what you're claiming?

_____

If you really want what you say you want, then what are you willing to do differently to get it?

_____

**Commit to what you want
and then start with the first item on your to-do list.**

Rushing?

Lorenzo grew up in Los Angeles. He hated it. For some reason, he figured Sacramento would be better. So he started saving up his money and told everyone he was leaving town as soon as he was able to put enough aside.

Finally, the day came when he could afford the move. This wasn't a sightseeing trip. Lorenzo wanted to get to his new home without delay. So he took the fastest least scenic route possible, stopping only once for gas.

Within a day of getting there, Lorenzo realized that he had made a mistake. He hated Sacramento as much as he hated LA.

Now what? He was in such a rush to get there that he didn't stop at any other towns along the way. All he learned was that he now hated two places instead of one.

Many people move through their lives in the same way that Lorenzo tried to escape Los Angeles. Their desires might be reasonable, but they're often rushing.

What if, instead of deciding upon a specific *destination* (like Sacramento), Lorenzo had chosen a *direction* (like generally north)?

Choosing a direction is less burdensome than choosing a destination. For instance, you might declare, "I want to get to

Sacramento as quickly as possible." You probably wouldn't say, "I want to get northwest as soon as possible."

When you have the perspective of heading in a direction, you allow yourself to enjoy the scenery and explore along the way.

If you ultimately get to Sacramento and don't like it, it's no problem because you probably discovered some wonderful towns en route.

Or if you do like Sacramento, that's wonderful. Your choice is affirmed because you can compare it with the abundance of towns you visited while on your journey.

Or if you fall in love with one of the towns prior to reaching Sacramento, that's great. Unpack the car.

A general direction, versus a fixed destination, offers more possibilities.

Slowing down gives you the opportunity to discover.

Slow down.

Enjoy the ride.

And take in the view.

What are you rushing to fix?

_____

What views are you missing?

_____

What enjoyment are you postponing?

_____

What benefits are you trying to receive too soon?

_____

Act with priorities instead of urgencies.

Take a breath.
Relax.
Start now.

"Time is but the stream I go a-fishing in.
I drink at it; but while I drink I see the sandy bottom
and detect how shallow it is.
Its thin current slides away, but eternity remains."
— Henry David Thoreau

Stupid?

"Are you calling me stupid?" Michael yelled.

"Is that a problem?" I responded.

"You bet it is!" Michael threatened. "How would you like it if I said the same about you?"

"It would be good to know. Do you think I'm stupid?"

"Yes."

"Okay. Thanks for telling me. It sounds like our conversation is over."

"You see? You don't like being called stupid, do you?" Michael gleefully declared while pointing his finger at me.

"No, really, Michael, it doesn't bother me. I'm just assuming there's no point in you getting advice from someone you think is stupid."

Michael didn't know how to respond.

"We're all stupid in certain areas of our life," I continued. "More areas than not, most likely. It really is good to know."

"But how can you accept it so calmly?" Michael challenged. "I don't really think you're stupid. I just said that to get a rise out of you."

"How did that work out?" I smiled.

"Not like I thought."

"Here's the thing, Mike. Like I said, most of us are stupid about a wide variety of things. I don't know much about brain surgery, physics, art, you name it. My knowledge is microscopic in comparison with humankind's. And that's being generous."

"That's true for all of us, I suppose," Michael contributed.

"I agree. So it's good to know what we don't know. Because those are the times we shouldn't be listening to ourselves. Those are the times to get more information."

"That makes sense. But what about what I said to you? How come you don't mind being called stupid? Were you just messing with me?"

"No, I wasn't messing with you. It really doesn't bother me."

"But how come?" Michael pressed. "If you're not stupid when I'm telling you you're stupid, then how can that not bother you? What if I'm just being an ass?"

"It doesn't matter whether you're being an ass or not, whether you're right or wrong, or whether you always think I'm stupid or just once in a while. If you are thinking that I am stupid, for however long you are thinking it, there's no point in my trying to convince you of anything unless you have a habit of being swayed by stupid people."

"But it's insulting," Michael persisted.

"No, it's not. You're announcing how you are feeling in the moment. You're giving me notice. I appreciate not having to waste my time."

"I still don't get it. How can it not bother you?"

"Three reasons. First, as I already said, there are lots of topics in which I am stupid. So I'm used to it. Second, there are times that I am temporarily stupid, like when I'm in pain or upset or tired."

"So you don't listen to yourself then?"

"Oh yeah. Never. I literally say to myself, 'Come back to me tomorrow.' I don't have conversations with myself when I can't be trusted."

"Wow, how did you learn that?"

"The hard way. Believe me."

Michael laughed.

"To finish answering your question," I continued, "the third reason being stupid doesn't bother me is that my overall disposition, my happiness in life, is not at all based on whether I'm smart or stupid or whether most people see me that way. I just need the people I love and respect to love me back."

"You didn't say 'respect you back'," Michael pointed out.

"You're right. I hope that they respect me in the areas in which I am worth respecting. And I really hope they don't respect or pretend to respect me in areas in which I don't deserve it. If they did, I'd get into a lot of trouble."

"What do you mean? Wouldn't it feel good?"

"No. It would feel fraudulent. And like I said, I could get into trouble if they were giving me undue credit."

"Give me an example."

"Well, if my friends and family respected my nonexistent fighting talents, I'd likely pick a fight with someone and get my ass kicked. If they respected my nonexistent singing talents, I'd be one of those guys who ends up on the weirdo reel of a television talent show audition."

"Yeah, some of those freaks are unbelievable," Michael laughed.

"Exactly," I agreed. "They're the perfect example of not facing reality and of having people around them who support their delusion."

Whether it's nonexistent intelligence or baseless talent, it's good to know reality.

So what if you're sometimes stupid? Just don't listen to yourself at those times. Either wait or talk to someone else instead.

If you are always stupid in a particular area, then always find someone credible to talk to.

There's no shame in admitting that you're stupid in the areas in which you are.

The problems arise when you don't.

In what areas are you unable to admit that you're stupid?

_____

Can you be okay with the fact that you don't know everything you think that you know?

_____

Whose intelligence are you denying?

_____

**Know where you're stupid
so that you can get whatever help you need.**

Inadequate?

Monty was always comparing himself to his friends and family.

"So, Monty," I asked, "what do you like better, oceans or mountains?"

"Uh, oceans," Monty hesitantly answered, wondering about my motives.

"Personally, I like mountains better."

"Okay. So what?" Monty demanded to know.

"Let's continue. List five things that make oceans great."

"Hmmm..." Monty pondered for a moment. "Well, you can surf and swim in them."

"All right."

"They host all sorts of fish life," Monty continued.

"Yep."

"They're so vast and deep that there are parts we have never explored."

"Perfect. Give me two more."

"You can sail on them to all parts of the world. And..."

Monty looked up as he put his finger to his mouth...

"Ah," he added, "and they're powerful."

"Excellent," I acknowledged. "Now it's my turn. Five cool things about mountains. They define valleys. You can see them from far away. You can hike and ski on them. Plant life and animals grow on them. And, let's see, they collect snow, which melts into water that flows into streams and rivers and lakes."

Monty nodded in agreement with a tentative smile on his face, still having no clue as to the point I was attempting to make.

"Now let's consider the not-so-good aspects of each of our choices," I said to Monty. "Name five things that aren't so pleasant about oceans."

"You can drown in them," Monty instantly replied. "They get polluted. It's easy to get lost on them. Sharks. And tsunamis."

"Okay," I accepted. "Mountains catch on fire. You can fall off them. Avalanches. They make it harder to travel on land. And planes can crash into them."

Monty agreed with my list while still wondering where I was headed.

"We could both come up with more positives and negatives," I pointed out. "But even though you chose oceans and I chose mountains, we would both agree that each is magnificent in its own right."

"Definitely," Monty confirmed.

"So, Monty, what's my point?"

"I don't have a clue."

"Although mountains and oceans have some elements in common, they are each spectacular despite not having what the other has. In other words, it's not necessary to have everything in order to be wonderful."

As humans, we forget that. We want every attribute under the sun, thinking that the more we have, the more spectacular we will be.

For me, that's the message in Genesis...

"Then [God] separated the light from the darkness."

As one, they were imperceptible.

"And God... separated the waters that were under the expanse from the waters that were above the expanse."

The creations needed to be distinguished from one another.

"Let the waters swarm with fish and other life. Let the skies be filled with birds of every kind."

Each creation has its function.

Before that...

"The earth was without form, and void..."

You don't have to be religious to appreciate the message. When everything has everything, there is nothing. The very definition of creation, as described by the Bible, was the separation of everything and nothing into something.

With specific distinctions, each has a purpose. We stay on land to hike, and we jump into water to swim.

You certainly can try to better yourself. It's great if you want to be the best you can be, so long as you're endeavoring to be more of who *you* are, not more of who someone else is.

How can you tell the difference? How do you know whether what you are attempting is consistent with who you are?

In many cases, it comes down to this... If you are an adult, your unfulfilled natural attributes are more likely diminished by something you *are* doing versus something you are *not* doing.

For instance, if you are not living up to your physical potential, you are likely engaged in some unhealthy activity that's hindering it. Maybe you're sleeping too late, playing too many video games, watching too much television, eating too much junk food, drinking too much, etc.

Likewise, if you are not living up to your career potential, maybe you're ignoring what needs to be done, arriving late, distracted, not learning your craft, complaining, belligerent, and so on.

If an attribute gets better by you stopping an aberrant behavior, then that's an attribute consistent with who you are meant to be.

To answer metaphorically, we are like blocks of wood. Within certain limits, we can change our finish, but not our grain. Walnut can never become birch or vice versa. And while we can stain most woods any color, certain colors don't take as well with certain types of woods.

Likewise, within limits, we can change our shape. But we have to recognize that some woods are harder than others.

Regardless of inherent limitations, every type of wood has its virtue. And just as it is with some pieces of wood, we can regard our knots as imperfections or as beautiful badges of uniqueness.

In some areas, we will be *deficient*. For these, our friends and family are wonderful sources.

In other areas, we will be *sufficient*. We can do what we need to do and optionally get some assistance.

In many areas, we might be *efficient*. We can easily handle what needs to be done on our own.

And in a few areas, we might be *proficient*. These are the ones that are most fun and rewarding to share with others.

No matter what, we are all inadequate at some things. That's a lot different from considering ourselves inadequate in general.

If oceans are spectacular despite not having all of the elements of mountains...

And mountains are spectacular despite not having all of the elements of oceans...

Then...

Why would you think yourself inadequate for not having everything that others might have?

In what ways do you believe yourself to be inadequate?

_____

Has someone tried and/or is someone still trying to turn you into something that you are not?

_____

Are you trying to do that?

_____

What would happen if you simply accepted who you are and appreciated what you had?

_____

**Consider yourself complete.
Now feel free to enhance yourself.**

Sophie sat perfectly erect with her arms crossed over her chest and both of her legs planted firmly on the ground.

For years, ever since Sophie was a child, she knew what she needed to be. She needed to be strong and independent.

It was the only way Sophie thought she could protect herself. The only way she could ever be happy. It hadn't worked yet, but Sophie was not dissuaded.

I asked Sophie and the entire group a question:

> "What are you missing by trying to be those things you think you should be, those things you decided as a child?"

> "You mean my being strong and independent?" Sophie inquired.

> "Yes. Exactly."

> "I could never give that up," Sophie defended with alarm.

> "You're not being asked to do that. But what are you missing by always trying to be strong?"

> Sophie answered after a thoughtful pause, "Allowing people to take care of me."

"Yes, that's true. What else?"

Sophie thought long and hard before realizing, "Intimacy."

"That's quite a loss, isn't it?"

Sophie sat silently.

"Let's do this... Sophie, go around the room and tell each person what you love about them."

After a short moment of hesitation, Sophie began. With tears in her eyes, she looked each person squarely in their eyes and shared the most beautiful of heartfelt sentiments.

In all my years of facilitating people, I never saw anyone so eloquent, connected, and loving.

Sophie finished. After a few moments of silence, I looked at Sophie and asked...

"How does it feel?"

"Wonderful," Sophie tearfully glowed.

I extended the question to the others.

"How about the rest of you? How did it feel?"

The recipients of Sophie's gifts revealed having sensations similar to Sophie's.

Cynthia spoke of feeling calm and grounded beyond anything she had ever experienced. Others talked about feeling seen for the first time.

Everyone was in tears.

"Sophie, there's something I want to make sure you have noticed," I imparted. "This sensation that you feel... this sensation that you generated all on your own... has nothing to do with being strong and independent."

Sophie began sobbing.

"And there's something I'd like the rest of you to notice," I continued. "Those wonderful sensations that you're experiencing... that warmth of being seen... those feelings of love and calmness from Sophie's words of acknowledgment... have nothing to do with one single thing that you have spent your entire life thinking you needed to have.

"You were acknowledged for who you are and for how you are really seen. Not for how you wish to be seen."

I waited for the realization to sink in.

"Those childhood conclusions, those pursuits, and all of those efforts were misguided. They have nothing to do with your happiness and everything to do with prolonging your pain.

"This is what it looks like to be seen for who you are.

"There is no greater gift than the gift of being, seeing, and loving your true self."

Are you finally ready to be your true self instead of who you have been wishing yourself to be?

Worry less about what you are
and enjoy who you are.

Tired?

Let's review...

As children, we take our observations and come to conclusions that have all of the intelligence, perception, insight, and wisdom one would expect from a five-year-old.

We develop solutions that we think will solve the problems that led to our pain.

We take all of these wants and call them needs.

We spend our lives in desperate pursuit.

We ignore who we are in favor of the unreal person we wish ourselves to be.

We ignore reality and anything that contradicts our childhood conclusions.

We think we're unique in our situation.

We engage in behavior that ensures our failure and/or alienates the people around us.

We behave as experts despite lacking any evidence that we know what we're doing.

We continue looking to ourselves for advice instead of others.

We don't take the advice we receive.

And then we wonder why we're stuck reliving our childhood pain.

Are you tired of it yet?

Let go to move forward.

Isolated?

Avi was a reasonably good college student with more ingenuity than book smarts. He wasn't an athlete, nor was he a klutz. He wasn't handsome, nor was he ugly. Wasn't popular nor unpopular. Didn't feel excluded or included. He somehow managed to be involved and on the periphery at exactly the same time, visible or invisible at will.

On paper, Tom was completely different from Avi and certainly not invisible. Actually, Tom was impossible to not notice. He was lean, muscular, and blond with off-the-charts athletic prowess and a cross of boyish charm and angelic qualities. There wasn't a single girl who wasn't attracted to Tom, and it would be difficult to quantify how much he enjoyed and took advantage of that fact.

While Avi was going unnoticed wearing long pants and buttoning his shirts one shy of the top button, Tom was wearing T-shirts and shorts and drawing stares wherever he went.

While Avi was deliberate in his movements, following a logical course from location to location, Tom seemed to spontaneously and effortlessly flow from one location to another.

And while Avi spent his summers working long hours at a high-tech company, Tom adventurously hitchhiked all over Europe, performed physical labor at farms across the countrysides, and climbed the Swiss Alps.

They became great friends.

The first time Avi and Tom hung out together, they went to see a horror film. Avi, knowing Tom's swashbuckling reputation, was surprised during the film to discover Tom with his knees hugged up to his chest, blocking his eyes at the sign of any gore.

Later, while at dinner, Avi was also surprised to discover that Tom sported a genius-level intelligence and was better read than most intellectuals twice his age. He was intense and thoroughly gentle. And he was no stranger to personal pain and heartache. It wasn't what Avi expected from the guy who was known to have boxed an armed mugger into submission.

Until they shared a meal, Avi didn't know that Tom, who had to be on guard for strange women groping his thighs whenever he walked in a crowd, was intensely guilty about all of his blessings. His brother was born with birth defects, and Tom couldn't help feeling bad for having double scoops of the virtues his brother so needed. And most surprisingly, Avi realized that Tom, a person who received so much adoration and with whom everyone wanted to be friends, was estranged from his family and felt alone.

Tom was surprised by what he found himself sharing. For some reason, he was saying things out loud that he had never said to anyone else. It was so comfortable, almost as if he and Avi were brothers. He had no idea that the slight Avi was so bold. That someone so intelligent was also so emotional. He had always figured that Avi was interesting, but he had no idea that Avi would be so interested. Avi had somehow become Tom's most trusted friend in a matter of moments. And for the very first time in his life, Tom felt what it was like to be seen from the inside out.

Avi wasn't inclined to travel the world and seek adventure. He loved that he could taste what it was like from the details that Tom vividly shared. At the same time, Tom felt anchored by Avi. He could travel the world knowing that he always had a home.

What a rich discovery the two enjoyed. They seemed so different, yet they were very much the same. Imagine the loss if either of them had believed in stereotypes.

It all began with a friendly conversation. Neither assumed that their differences would be a deal breaker. They talked, became friends, and discovered the benefits of what each of them had to offer.

To whatever degree we set ourselves apart from others, whether through the insecurity of entitlement, overrating our abilities, acting as if we have virtues we don't have, denying or resenting the virtues of others, we leave ourselves a little emptier.

Whenever we think that no one knows our sorrows, that no one can understand our pains, that no one can feel as deeply, and whatever other bragging rights we claim to our suffering, we leave ourselves isolated.

In our distancing, we inflict upon ourselves one of our greatest fears: the despair of being alone.

You might be great, but you're not so special.

You might be wounded, but you're not unique.

Be thankful for that.

What people have you isolated yourself from because you think they're too different from you?

_____

What have you declared is something that no one but you can understand?

_____

Join the rest of us in the world.

Ill-Advised?

If you have some areas of your life that you are working on and aren't just reading this book for pleasure, you probably realize that you need a perspective outside yourself.

If you are going to ask for assistance, you want to be sure that the person you're asking is credible. So here are some questions to consider:

1. Do you need to talk to someone? In general, having a trusted family member, friend, and/or professional is a great thing. In addition to "trusted", also make sure they're "trustworthy".

2. Are you seeking an opinion or advice? If you want opinions, then you can seek multiples and then make your selection from the most credible people. On the other hand, if you're going for advice, as I am defining the word, then you want to go to the most credible person and do what they suggest.

3. Can you properly consider the advice? The best way to do that, assuming you don't need to take an urgent action, is to spend twenty-four hours pretending that the person is correct. As your objections surface, just tell yourself to raise the concern in twenty-four hours. This technique will allow the other perspectives, the ones consistent with the advice, to emerge.

4. Do you need business assistance? If so, make sure the person has a respectable track record in an arena as close to yours as possible.

5. Do you need emotional assistance? The same criterion about one's track record applies.

6. Can you relate to the person from whom you are seeking advice? There needs to be a good connection. You want to feel heard and understood. You want someone who gives you the feeling of being interested and on your side.

7. Are they dated? Some things never change, but you want to be sure you're talking with someone who's in touch with how the world is, not only how it used to be.

8. Do they appear interested? Years of experience is wonderful, but you also want to be sure the person is as vital as you need to be in your pursuit. Think about the energy that coaches have on the sidelines. You need someone who will inspire you.

9. Do they subscribe to other disciplines? This could be any number of perspectives from literature, Buddhism, sports, interests outside of their profession, etc. You want someone who is curious and not dogmatic.

10. Does this person make you feel safe? You want someone who is direct, not critical. And you want them to be honest while remaining heartfelt.

11. Are they in competition with you? If so, run.

12. Have they failed at their previous pursuit? Be sure that they have evolved into a new calling, as opposed to being begrudgingly engaged in their backup plan.

13. Do you trust the person who recommended them? You want to be sure that this person has a level of discernment that you trust, that you have similar tastes, and that you have witnessed an evolution and growth in them, especially if they're sending you to the person who allegedly provided them assistance.

14. How is the person dressed? You want them to be appropriate to the circumstance, like a businessperson in business attire, a coach in athletic attire, etc.

    You want to be sure that their manner of dress is consistent with the results you want in your own life. For example, if you're seeking a sense of order, you won't get that from someone who's slovenly.

    You want to see whether their style of dress illustrates their comfort with their own place in life versus an older person trying to look too young and hip, an out-of-shape person dressing in something too tight, and anyone whose attire is too revealing.

    In essence, you want someone's style of dress to be consistent with everything you're looking for. Most importantly, you want to be sure that it's not distracting to you in any way.

15. Are they resentful of other people you have talked to? If so, run.

16. Are they open to all of the criteria covered in the previous questions? If not, run.

Talking aside,
find some time
to hold someone's hand.

Sabotaging?

If you are not moving forward in one or more areas of your life, there's a very good chance you are being sabotaged. On occasion, the interference might be coming from someone else. But most likely, your sabotage is self-generated.

The following is a list of the specific mistakes, one or more of which you are probably making.

In one or more areas of your life...

1. You don't notice that you need advice.

2. You notice it, but you don't admit it.

3. You admit it, but you don't seek it.

4. You wait until it's too late and seek the advice after the fact.

5. You go to the wrong person.

6. You argue as if you're credible or engage in some other behavior (using anger or sympathy, for example) to make the advice harder to deliver.

7. You omit details that make the advice less effective.

8. You resent what you hear.

9. You forget what you're told.

10. You ignore the advice.

11. You misrepresent the advice when explaining it to others.

12. You find someone to contradict it.

13. You don't act upon it.

14. You follow it narrowly.

15. You misapply it.

16. You follow it inconsistently.

17. You prematurely stop following it.

18. You don't follow up with the person who gave the advice, so you don't get assistance in refining it.

19. You don't acknowledge where the advice came from, sometimes pretending that you thought of it.

20. You pretend or act as if you never needed it.

If you are stuck, you are doing one or more of the things on the previous list.

To get unstuck...

A. Ask yourself whether you are committed to having and/or accomplishing what you say you want.

If the answer is no, then congratulations on telling the truth. No need to read further.

If the answer is yes, then...

B. Reread the numbered list from the previous pages, starting with the very first item.

C. As soon as you find the item or items that you are engaging in, do the opposite. For instance, if you're not admitting that you need advice, then start admitting it.

D. If you can't stop the behavior, then ask yourself again whether you are committed to having what you claim.

Without a doubt, the less you engage in any of the behaviors from the numbered list, the more success you will have.

**Being stuck is a state of mind
built from stale thoughts
and misguided commitments
to the ineffective.**

**Look up.
Walk forward.
And enjoy the view.**

Loving?

When I was in my late teens, I escorted my grandmother to a convalescent home to visit a friend of hers.

Walking through the first dismal corridor, we passed a nasty old woman with a horrible disposition.

After gaining a reasonable distance from her, I whispered to my grandmother...

> "Wow. She grew old and crotchety."

> "No," my grandmother corrected. "As you are at seven, you are at seventy. She has always been old and crotchety."

Those words have never left me. I don't know whether my grandmother was right about the specifics of the age, but the message remains true. We set ourselves on life's course with a point of view. And if we're lucky, we see some alternatives along the way.

That crotchety old woman might have seen a lot of pain in her life, not to mention inflicted a fair amount upon others. Nevertheless, she undoubtedly came by her disposition honestly. But so have most people.

I couldn't tell you how many conversations I've had with those seeking my advice. Obviously, it's no small number. But I can tell you this: I have never changed a single person. I don't have that power.

At best, I can help someone see parts of themselves that might have gone unnoticed. Accept parts of themselves they might have rejected. And hopefully appreciate parts of themselves that deserve their love.

My grandmother regularly told me...

> "When you have your health, you have everything."

Despite both my parents being sick throughout my childhood, I never fully appreciated that wisdom until I was older.

Not everyone is blessed with good health. Some squandered theirs. Others never had it to begin with. But that's just the physical. Important, yes. But there's more.

There's our emotional well-being and our character. And in that regard...

If you have the good fortune of being loved and the even better fortune of having people to love, then you are truly rich.

And if you can treat yourself kindly and show others the same consideration, you will have a treasure.

Everything else is optional.

It's all frosting on the cake.

Love.
Be loved.

Be thankful.
Be kind.

Be happy.

Alphabetical Index

www.ingramcontent.com/pod-product-compliance
Lightning Source LLC
LaVergne TN
LVHW051515080426
835509LV00017B/2069